AF305253

THE
DAY AFTER

THE DAY AFTER

How to Wield Power in a Post-Trump World

BRIAN TYLER COHEN

HARPER

An Imprint of HarperCollins Publishers

HarperCollins books may be purchased for educational, business, or sales promotional use. For information, please email the Special Markets Department at SPsales@harper collins.com.

hc.com

FIRST EDITION

Library of Congress Cataloging-in-Publication Data has been applied for.

ISBN 978-0-06-349510-4

Printed in the United Kingdom

26 27 28 29 CPI 10 9 8 7 6 5 4 3 2

TO MY PARENTS
FOR THE BOTTOMLESS WELL OF LOVE,
SUPPORT, AND ENCOURAGEMENT

CONTENTS

Foreword

Every day we are reminded of the terrible consequences of the 2024 election. Donald Trump's return to office has been characterized by an aged autocrat surrounded by cowards and sycophants. Any pretense that there are guardrails has been disproven. There are no adults in the room.

His cabinet and those in the White House see their roles as facilitating his illegal and unconstitutional actions. They shower praise on him as if he were an insecure despot. They execute his wishes and cater to his every whim as if he were a powerful dictator. They are the court jesters in Trump's pretend kingdom.

Even worse are the Republicans in Congress. Under our system of government, they are supposed to put their constituents' interests first and jealously guard their legislative power and prerogatives. They are supposed to check executive overreach and balance the president's power with the powers they uniquely control.

Instead, Congressional Republicans act as though they are part of the administration rather than members of a coequal branch of government. They tried to forfeit their taxing power—part of which is the power to impose tariffs—to Trump, until the Supreme Court stepped in. They permitted Trump to take the nation to war without a congressional declaration. But worst of all, perhaps, has been their refusal to conduct meaningful oversight of the corruption and abuses committed by Trump, his friends and family, and the administration.

The Republican Party—once the Grand Old Party—is now little more than a vessel for Trump's cult of personality. It has been gutted of any meaningful role in national politics other than to effectuate his policies. It has no platform other than what Trump posts on social media. It supports the candidates he tells it to support and spends money at his behest.

As damaging as the collapse of governmental checks has been to our democracy, the retreat of our largest private institutions has been even more devastating. Early in his tenure, Trump made clear he wanted to neutralize the two pillars of American democracy that could hold him to account—law firms and media companies.

When Trump targeted the nation's largest law firms, many people assumed they would fight back. Instead, while a handful stood tall, most fell into line. The worst cut deals with Trump to provide him with hundreds of millions of dollars worth of free legal services. But many more simply stayed silent while the rule of law was attacked.

The large media corporations that promised to hold power to account are instead settling bogus claims that put money in his pocket. They have proven that democracy can die in the full light of day just as easily as in the darkness of night.

If all of this sounds deeply pessimistic, it is not meant to be. Yes, the system is broken. However, if we only focus on how to fix it, we will miss the big opportunity that awaits us. No matter what happens in 2028, we will not return to the governmental and political systems of the past.

In many respects, the failure of the Biden era was a belief that our democracy could be restored to what it was before Trump. It can *not* be. More importantly, that should not be our ultimate goal.

Instead, those in the pro-democracy movement should focus on what comes next. We must not seek to restore the past, but insist that it be replaced with something bolder and built for the future. Our goal should be the transformation of our institutions, not merely their restoration.

Shortly after Trump's election in 2024, I wrote about the need to move beyond a "resistance." The problem with that term is that it is both reactive and temporally limited. A resistance is necessarily built to push back against something, rather than to expand to fill a vacuum left by the absence of power. It will also, therefore, be limited to the period in which there is something to resist.

For the same reason, I am skeptical of any plan that begins in 2029 and lasts only four years. Many of the structural changes needed must start now. And many of the policies will take much longer to enact and implement.

Take media, for example. We need to build a vibrant, independent media ecosystem now. It cannot wait for the next election or the next movement leader. Yes, Democratic candidates need to embrace it—but we must build it before that will become possible.

For the last several years Brian Tyler Cohen and I have had an ongoing conversation around these issues on our *Democracy Watch* YouTube podcast. It was during those conversations—and others off-air—that Brian first outlined to me some of the arguments at the heart of this book. I remember thinking: *Someone needs to write this down.* He did.

Together we have spent countless hours documenting in real time what Trump and his enablers are doing to our elections and our institutions. Week after week, Brian has shown a remarkable ability to cut through the noise and explain what is actually at stake in language that reaches people where they are. This book does the same thing in written form—and it could not come at a more critical moment.

Rebuilding governmental institutions will take years—more likely decades—to design, test, and implement. So too will the development of new lines of jurisprudence and legal thought. In fact, most of the assumptions underlying our past policies may be no longer correct.

We must challenge them to determine whether they will be ready to meet the moment ahead or are simply ideas from the past.

None of this will be easy. There will be disagreements among the pro-democracy camp on policies, strategies, and tactics. That is a good thing. We need to foster open debate and disagreement. We need to be a big tent of ideas and approaches.

This book, and others like it, are part of that process. That is why I wrote this foreword, and why I encourage you to not simply read it but to wrestle with it and debate it in your own minds before drawing conclusions. If you do, you will find it will make you think and inspire you to act.

I have watched Brian do this work up close. As a part of our work and our friendship we have pushed each other to think harder about what democracy requires of us right now. This book reflects that same rigor and urgency. Brian does not ask you to simply resist. He asks you to imagine—and then build—what will come next. That is exactly the right ask for this moment.

The fight for democracy is the challenge of our generation. We all need to do our part. With this book, Brian Tyler Cohen has made exactly the kind of contribution this movement needs—not a eulogy for what we have lost, but a blueprint for what we can build.

—Marc Elias
March 2026

Prologue

It never used to feel so cold in Mar-a-Lago. There was an empty chill that came not just from the overworked air-conditioning. The weather outside was still delightful in late January 2029, the usual damp warmth that brought all those old snowbirds to Palm Beach. But inside, the old source of heat—the anxious crowds of influence peddlers and stargazers—had slipped away, week by week as the battleground states had fallen one by one.

The unlit chandeliers and vacant sofas were the only witnesses to the old man in the white polo shirt tucked into his black pants hobbling through the darkened room, his phone pressed close to his pale, dry lips. He refused to lean on a cane or walker, even though he had desperately needed one since his eighty-second birthday the previous summer. The last thing he wanted was to look as old and weak as Joe Biden had in his final months in office. So he limped and shuffled around the antiques, consumed by his calls to the businessmen, advisers, and sycophants about the pathetic campaign run by his vice president. *I should never have trusted Don Jr.'s advice. Vance was always a fake, a fraud, a fucking Yale lawyer. My people knew he wasn't MAGA. He said I was America's Hitler. What the hell is he? He's America's Loser. His name isn't even JD.*

He thought about pushing his Supreme Court to stretch the Constitution a little more. There was always a domestic insurrection or alien invasion that could have called for a few more years in the Oval Office. But as it turned out, losing power wasn't what stung him most. Like his thinning hairline and fattening waistline, he could always cover that up. Power was perception. Power was money. And he had made billions.

No, what was worse than leaving the White House was the absence of eyeballs. With every passing day it was getting harder and harder to keep his gold-plated grip on public attention. There was so much slop out there on social media, so many jaw-dropping videos that looked so real. In truth, on Truth Social, he'd lost the power to shock and awe some time before, around the 2026 midterms that had swept away his fragile hold on Congress. The economy had gone sideways for three years, with only the AI billionaires feeling flush. The MAGA party was over; the job had turned into a grind. The prosecutions of his enemies— James Comey, Adam Schiff, Letitia James—had fallen apart. The tariffs had been taken down; first by the courts, then by necessity. The crypto bubble had burst a couple of billion in meme coins. The Middle East still burned, and the Nobel Peace Prize had never landed.

Still, he had left his mark. There was the new triumphal Trump Arch opposite the Lincoln Memorial; the new Trump ballroom that dominated the old White House; and a huge Qatari plane parked at Palm Beach International Airport at great expense. All he needed to do was raise a billion dollars for the brand-new skyscraper in Miami that would be home to his presidential library and luxury spa hotel.

Everyone was vying to be the next Donald John Trump, but they were only pale imitations. He would make sure to remind anyone and everyone that the Big Dog overshadowed all the little chihuahuas.

* * *

Back in the nation's capital, the newly elected Democratic president stared at a pile of executive orders ready for signature on the Resolute

Desk. The Oval Office still smelled of fresh paint from the rapid switchover on inauguration day. Outside there was a steady beat of metal against metal as the construction crews dismantled the viewing platforms for the inaugural parade. Dismantling the last four years would be much louder.

Despite all the very real fears of mob violence, foreign interference, and fake video reports about fake votes, the results of the presidential election of 2028 had been certified. That might have been the result of JD Vance's unbridled arrogance. Defeat had been so unthinkable that he had waited too long to embrace fully the 2028 Big Lie conspiracy. It was too little, too late.

The relative ease of the transition had passed over Washington like some political anesthetic. So many of the capital's traditionalists felt a long-lost sense of calm. After four years of turmoil and terror, rumor and repression, corruption and criminality, the pain was receding. Life *could* return to normal. Institutions *could* be rebuilt. Elected officials *could* speak their minds, stand on their principles, reclaim the constitutional powers bequeathed by the founders. Bipartisanship, civility, and the truth lay right around the corner. The rest of the world had celebrated November's results in the streets of London, Paris, Tokyo, and Beijing. World leaders could sleep soundly once again, banishing their nightmarish fears of alliances broken, commerce disrupted, diplomacy destroyed. Trump had talked about slapping his illegal tariffs on the world as Liberation Day. Now America's allies were partying like they had truly been liberated from a long international nightmare.

Inside the White House, however, the conflict had not come to an end. The new president faced a stark choice between two rival sets of advisers. On one side were the Washington veterans. They had grown up on Capitol Hill and congressional campaigns, and their networks had proved to be invaluable with donors, endorsements, ad agencies, and traditional media. They knew how to lock in convention delegates, schmooze the interest groups, and whip votes. They believed, deep in their bones, that it was time to heal the fractured nation, bind up the wounds of the Trump years, turn the page on a painful past, and begin to rebuild. They had signed up for the restoration of the Washington they knew. They wanted to shy away from the politics of conflict and confrontation.

On the other side were the insurgent upstarts, who were gunning for the fight of a lifetime, the rejects and newcomers who had failed to get a job on one of the many campaigns led by purple-state governors and senators—or had never wanted one of those jobs in the first place. They had carried the torch for the newly inaugurated president when the candidate had been unsure of victory in the first primary states. They didn't believe in the status quo, because they had no trust or place in it. The voters wanted change, and they embodied the forces of change. The best way to restore democracy was not to return to the old ways of 2024 or even 2016; it was to build a fortress of democracy that the next brand of neo-fascist MAGA heads would be unable to destroy. Surely the biggest lesson of the Biden presidency had been to extinguish the naive belief that once there was a Democratic president again, the world would just revert back to normal.

Caught between the old guard and the new, between the traditionalists and the reformers, between the middle and the muscle, was the forty-eighth president of the United States. Alone at the Resolute Desk, the new president stared at the walls of the Oval Office, where all the fake gold decorations had been stripped and shipped down to Florida, and wondered what, besides the paint job, would have to be done to renovate this office.

* * *

Here's the reality. We're not teetering on the brink of autocracy; we've fallen off the cliff of democracy, and we need to be ready for what comes next. One of the main reasons Trump 2.0 damaged these United States so much more than Trump 1.0 was because they planned for it. In detail, in unison. Project 2025, which candidate

Trump made such a transparent pretense of disavowing, was not some cut-and-paste job the interns had slapped together; it was the culmination of years—no, decades—of planning and patient building, the kind of planning that Trump himself couldn't manage if it involved a casino in Atlantic City or a high-rise hotel in Riyadh. He was the perfect host for a virus that infected not just our country but half the world. To cure the patient will need more than hydroxychloroquine or ivermectin or—dare I say—Tylenol. It will take a clear-eyed diagnosis of how we got sick and how powerful the virus remains. We need to learn from our weaknesses and from their strengths. Like the best vaccines, the ones that scientifically save lives, we'll need to mimic the virus so we can beat it with our own natural defenses. Because after four years of wanton vandalism and corruption, it will take guts to do this. And it will take power; not just winning power but wielding it effectively, once progressives have gotten it back.

This is no time for the fainthearted. You can't chew your fingernails, worrying about whether the old guard will like or respect what you're doing. Or whether the other side will cry foul when they are forced to contend with the same exercise of power they once enjoyed. In the fight to save what's left of our democratic republic, we will need to break the rules—because the rules have already been broken, repeatedly and shamelessly, by the corrupt opponents of our own Constitution.

That's not just a job for our elected officials, although they carry more of the burden than their voters do. It's also our job, the job of each and every one of us. What are we going to do to seize this moment, to recognize the gravity of our times, beyond shaking our heads at the news? How will we exercise our power as citizens while we still have it? Because it's not good enough to share a video about yet another ICE raid on the streets. When you're face to face with the secret police on your sidewalk, you need to stand up for those being terrorized in the name of Trump. It's not good enough to applaud the establishment candidates who promise that everything can get back to normal. When you vote in the primaries, you will need to select candidates who understand the urgency of the moment we're in. And when the day after Trump finally arrives, it won't be good enough to get back to your old life—because the repair and rebuilding of our communities and country are the work of millions of people, not just members of Congress.

It's time to look at power with the cold, clear eyes of the great Italian analyst of how to rule. Niccolò Machiavelli wrote five hundred years ago that a leader needs to be a mixture of a fox and a lion: a fox to recognize the traps and a lion to frighten the wolves. This is the playbook for the progressives who are the foxes and lions of a world that Trump changed forever.

1

The Long Game

If you're shocked by the speed of descent of our democracy, you've probably seen the easy explanation of why Trump 2.0 is so much worse than Trump 1.0. The pundits say that Trump learned from his last time around: He now knows how to wield power, punish enemies, and purge the establishment that slowed him down. All of which is true, but it's only part of the story—a story that stretches back several decades. Because the broader right-wing movement also learned its lessons and saw its greatest opportunity in the second coming of Donald Trump.

The project didn't start in 2025. It took a half century of plotting and scheming, but it finally came to pass on the fourth attempt. You see, Donald J. Trump is just the endpoint of a very, very long conservative campaign to wield power for the profit of the few. What started with the imperial presidency of Richard Nixon found its popular expression in Ronald Reagan, its military force in George W. Bush, and its brazen lawlessness in a reality TV star. Autocracy is the just cost of doing business, and it's one the oligarchy is more than ready to pay.

To understand how we got here and what we must do now, we need to get our heads around the world the baby boomers lived in.

Yes, the actual baby boomers. Today they range in age from a spritely sixtysomething (a mere fetus in the halls of the Capitol) to one of the many eightysomethings who are now clinging to power. That would include the current and last presidents, the current and last Senate majority leaders, and the current and last Senate minority leaders. They grew up in the 1950s, in a country that would soon fade away in a series of liberal reforms that shaped the world we know today.

What did that country look like seventy years ago? It was chronically, deeply divided by Jim Crow racial laws that systematically oppressed people of color. It was chronically, deeply divided by a patriarchy that kept women at home, with little control of their reproductive health. Large corporations were free to pollute our rivers and lie to their own customers. The culture was so monochrome that it was shaken by a white man singing Black songs by the name of Elvis Presley. Where there was dissent, it had little purpose. The most shocking movie of the decade quite literally summed up the mood: *Rebel Without a Cause.*

That's not to say that the politics of the time were stable. Far from it. At the start of the Cold War, amid the existential fear of Soviet expansion and nuclear weapons, people were easily spooked. If the Commies weren't already here, the UFOs certainly were. It was an era ripe for a demagogue who peddled conspiracies and smears in a fake campaign against the supposed enemies within; a demagogue who terrorized US government, business, and culture; a demagogue who manipulated right-wing media, cozied up to neo-Nazis, and sought sweetheart deals for his cronies. In other words, it looked much like the America of Donald Trump's dreams.

It was Joseph McCarthy who first created the Trump-shaped space in our politics. The Wisconsin senator did not invent the threat of Communist spies in the United States. He just preyed on Americans' fears of the unknown to stoke up a supposedly patriotic mob to root out a vast wave of enemies that did not exist. The Reds under the bed were the criminal migrants of today. Many Americans were happy to play along with the fearmongering, just as they are today. The Dwight D.

Eisenhower administration even used the fear of Communist infiltration to justify the first mass deportations of Mexican immigrants using military tactics: Operation Wetback. The name says it all. Its agents swept up Latino workers, including American citizens, detaining them in dismal conditions, and dumping them into remote parts of Mexico with no food, water, or contact with their families.

McCarthy didn't start the Red Scare or the witch hunts; he just perfected them. The stage was set by the Hollywood blacklist and the smears of the House Un-American Activities Committee. Popular culture, they claimed, had been infiltrated by Communists, or at least by so-called fellow travelers. Walt Disney himself said that the Communist threat in Hollywood was real. Ronald Reagan claimed that there were Communist-style tactics taking place in the actors' union he led at the time. The result was a purge of actors, directors, writers, and musicians based on conspiracy theories and innuendos, fueled by Congress and conservative pressure groups. For right-wing zealots, the mainstream media has always been disloyally liberal, promoting un-American values such as diversity, equality, and inclusion.

McCarthy took those culture wars deep inside the federal government. It was like today's deep-state conspiracy, only full of Reds. The senator rose to infamy by claiming that the State Department was "infested with Communists" and that he had in his possession a list of 205 names of them. It was dramatic and specific, and there was a tiny kernel of fact in the scare tactic: Some two hundred State Department employees had undergone security checks at the time. The only problem was that they had, in fact, been cleared. But why ruin a good story with facts? It was a bit like claiming that Latin American countries are emptying their prisons to flood our borders with criminals. All it takes is one undocumented immigrant committing one serious crime for the big lie to take hold.

McCarthy claimed that there were numerous conspiracies inside the federal government, a cabal of Communists, homosexuals, and their sympathizers and protectors. He suggested that President Harry Truman was a drunk and should be impeached. He accused General

George C. Marshall, Jr., who had led the reconstruction of Europe after the war and won the Nobel Peace Prize, of treason because Communists had taken control of China.

All he needed to weaponize his demagoguery was the chairman's position in a Senate subcommittee. There he could hire his own henchmen. Among them was a twenty-year-old lawyer he named as his chief counsel. Roy Cohn had gained attention as a prosecutor of Julius and Ethel Rosenberg, two Soviet spies who had been executed for passing secrets to the enemy—despite the weak case against Ethel, the mother of two children. Cohn would go on to become the first mentor of and chief fixer for one Donald J. Trump as the latter started his real estate career in New York.

McCarthy and Cohn started investigating supposed Communists at the Voice of America, the radio network designed to undermine actual Communists and autocrats, which has now been shut down by Trump's henchmen. One radio engineer committed suicide after testifying in front of the committee. They moved on to banning supposedly pro-Communist books in State Department libraries. Then they attacked the clergy for harboring Communists, because when you think about it, Christ was suspiciously concerned with the welfare of the poor. Finally, they investigated the US Army itself in televised hearings that lasted thirty-six days.

Tell me if this sounds familiar.

It didn't really matter that they couldn't find actual Communists. For those who believed in the norms of American democracy, there was shock and disbelief at the way McCarthy and Cohn used the tools of Congress to undermine some of the foundations of democracy: a commitment to the truth, the presumption of innocence until proven guilty, support for those dedicated to public service, all of it wrapped in the flag of patriotic concern about foreign enemies who also peddled lies, framed the innocent, and corrupted public servants.

Wasn't America supposed to be different from its enemies? One of the most famous lines against McCarthy was from Joseph Welch, the army's chief lawyer, who said after one more outrageous smear, "Have you no sense of decency, sir, at long last?"

No, they had no sense of decency. They still don't. (I wrote a book about this called *Shameless: Republicans' Deliberate Dysfunction and the Battle to Preserve Democracy*, and the title continues to prove true.) Then as now, the vast majority of decent Americans had no idea how to respond—beyond expressing their deep sense of shock.

A noxious soup of smears, bullying, false victimhood, vicious counterattacks, media distraction, legal intimidation, and empty promises: The McCarthy playbook is now positively presidential. It's a projection of power when your position is especially weak.

* * *

As stuck in their ways as they seem today, the boomers who are now our leaders came of age in a revolutionary time: the 1960s. It was a decade that was shaped by the Kennedy reforms and assassinations, the civil rights movement and segregationist violence, the Vietnam War and antiwar defiance. There were literally revolutions and coups taking place around the world. Regimes fell in Cuba, Brazil, Syria, and Iraq. Across Africa and the Caribbean, newly independent countries were emerging from a century of empire. The world was changing before their eyes.

At the same time, American culture and values were transforming into what we know today, from music and fashion to language and literature. It wasn't just sex, drugs, and rock'n'roll—as important, enduring, and enjoyable as they are. Alongside birth control and abortion rights came women's liberation. Alongside civil rights came the Stonewall riots and gay rights. The counterculture pushed back on rampant corporate power. Rachel Carson's writing sparked an entire environmental movement. As primitive as it may look today, the technological breakthroughs of the time were step changes in what the world could imagine: from passenger jets to space travel, from communication satellites to color TVs and ATMs.

Those fundamental shifts were mirrored in our politics and in laws that changed the course of the whole country. The Civil Rights Act of 1964 banned discrimination based on race, religion, and sex. It integrated schools, hotels, restaurants, theaters, and swimming pools. It created the Equal Employment Opportunity Commission to ban discrimination at work, including in hiring, promotions, and pay. It was the most sweeping civil rights legislation since the post–Civil War era of Reconstruction. It was followed the next year by the Voting Rights Act, which stopped the vote-denying traditions of literacy tests and poll taxes, especially in the Deep South.

That same year, 1965, Congress passed Medicare and Medicaid into law, creating two of the most popular government programs to this day. That same Congress enacted the Department of Housing and Urban Development to support the elderly, disabled, and war veterans, as well as build community centers in low-income neighborhoods. Those neighborhoods received additional funding for schools from education legislation.

It was the year the United States finally abolished the racist immigration quotas that had been in place since the 1920s, ending the system that had intentionally banished the people of southern and eastern Europe. The 1965 Immigration and Nationality Act prioritized family reunions and the entry of skilled workers to help the US economy.

Congress even sought to change the culture, creating the National Endowment for the Arts and, two years later, the Corporation for Public Broadcasting. That led directly to the birth of PBS television and NPR radio stations, based on the old-fashioned belief that it was good for Americans to watch and listen to educational and informational programming. To that end, it created strong safeguards against political interference.

Above all, the culture shifted decisively in favor of feminism. Betty Friedan's 1963 book *The Feminine Mystique* helped break the dam holding women back from the workplace and confining them to motherhood and domestic duties. The book sold 3 million copies and was published in the same year that President John F. Kennedy signed the Equal Pay Act into law. By the end of the decade, the women's liberation movement was born, pushing for legalized abortion and the Equal Rights Amendment to the Constitution. In 1960, women made up one-third of the workforce. A generation later, in 1990, they made up almost half. The world as we knew it today was born in the 1960s, and the reactionary forces of conservative, corporate America have resented it ever since.

It's no coincidence that Charlie Kirk liked to say that women should go to college to get an "MRS" degree—to find a husband. He said that to a fourteen-year-old young woman interested in political journalism at a Young Women's Leadership Conference in Dallas just a couple of months before his assassination. His wife, Erika, told the young women at the conference to deprioritize their careers and start having babies as soon as possible. That's the same kind of thinking embraced by the neo-Nazi Nick Fuentes in his chummy chitchat with Tucker Carlson in October 2025. You can call their ideal woman a tradwife if you like. But they're talking about returning to the role women had before the 1960s.

MAGA propagandists might tell you that the Trump agenda is about freedom or patriotism or bringing down the price of eggs. You might even think it's just a bunch of demented brain farts from a very old man who struggles to read from a teleprompter. Except that's not true (notwithstanding his obvious struggles with a teleprompter). When they talk about returning this country to what it used to be— making America "great" *again*—they mean turning back the clock to the decades before the 1960s, when you could discriminate freely and widely based on race, religion, and sex. You could do that as a hotel owner, a state official, or the federal government. You could keep foreigners out of the country if they didn't look right to you or practiced what you thought was the wrong religion. You didn't have to spend money on communities that struggled to make ends meet, because you could also stop them from voting if you wanted to. And you didn't need to worry about the culture or the news that people consumed because it was all funded by your corporate buddies. In other words, they were good times for wealthy white men.

It was bad enough that Congress and the White House had been reshaping the nation in line with the hippie, drug-addled world known as Liberal America. But it was truly disastrous for the reactionary, conservative forces—the segregationists and Klansmen, the far-right John Birch Society members, the anti-Communist McCarthyite witch-hunters—that the courts repeatedly sided with these newfangled values of liberty and equality. It might have been self-evident to the signers of the Declaration of Independence that all men were created equal, but you didn't have to include every American unless the courts forced you to. Which was what they did.

Take women's rights, for instance. In 1965, the Supreme Court ruled against a Connecticut law that stopped married couples from using contraceptives. The Court blocked government restrictions on birth control based on the right to privacy—the idea that the government couldn't tell you what to do in your bedroom, just as it couldn't storm into your home without a judicial warrant. The case was brought in the name of Estelle Griswold, the executive director of Planned Parenthood in the state. The same right to privacy was extended to unmarried couples in 1972, and then the right to abortion in a 1973 case you may have heard of, *Roe v. Wade*. It extended all the way to the right to same-sex marriage in 2015.

When the Trump Supreme Court struck down *Roe*, its members said that the right to privacy did not extend to abortion. This from a bunch of hard-line conservatives who would surely faint if a Democratic president tried to raid Mar-a-Lago without due process. You see, due process lies at the heart of the right to privacy. It's fundamental to the Constitution as we know it. It comes from the Fourteenth Amendment, which was perhaps the biggest legal change to the country after the Civil War. It guarantees equal protection for all citizens, which was the bedrock principle for integrating schools, allowing interracial marriage and affirmative action, and stopping race-based gerrymandering.

Trump's assault on democracy is a means to an end. It's not the purpose of the project. The goal is to turn back the clock and take away your rights.

* * *

The 1960s were an unmitigated disaster for the Republican Party, especially the abject failure of the Barry Goldwater campaign in 1964. Goldwater was the archetype for what would follow: a norm-breaking, gun-slinging hawk, beloved by the far Right. The Arizona senator hated Franklin Delano Roosevelt's New Deal and opposed the Civil Rights Act of 1964 because it had stopped racist hiring practices and segregation in the private sector. He was such a hard-line anti-Communist that he thought nuclear weapons should be dropped onto Vietnam. He even believed that field commanders in Europe should be able to deploy smaller tactical nukes without presidential approval. As he said during his convention speech, "I would remind you that extremism in the defense of liberty is no vice. And let me remind you also that moderation in the pursuit of justice is no virtue!"

Goldwater was the star of the Republican Party, its dream candidate, willing and ready to take on the liberal northern wing of the party, the newly pro–civil rights Democrats, and all those Communists around the world. In an election barely a year after Kennedy's assassination, Goldwater lost in a landslide to Lyndon B. Johnson, winning just five states in the Deep South as well as his home state of Arizona. Those southern states had not voted Republican since the end of Reconstruction in 1877. Goldwater's campaign slogan was "In your heart, you know he's right." The Johnson campaign crafted its own version: "In your guts, you know he's nuts."

What emerged from the wreckage of Goldwater's campaign led directly to the sixty-year-long project to dismantle the progress of that era and, along the way, what we understand as American democracy. Goldwater's campaign leaned heavily on a group of advisers and speechwriters drawn from the top staff of the American Enterprise

Institute (AEI), a right-wing think tank established and funded by executives from some of the biggest corporations in the country at the time. AEI would go on to become the incubator for some of the most powerful officials under George W. Bush.

Goldwater's legal adviser on his campaign was William Rehnquist, a young lawyer who worked for his campaign manager. When Richard Nixon won the presidency in 1968, he became a key part of the right-wing plan to take over the Supreme Court and roll back the liberalism of the 1960s. Rehnquist was assistant attorney general at the heart of a politicized Justice Department that investigated a sitting Supreme Court justice, Abe Fortas. Fortas was hounded into stepping down from the Court in Nixon's first year in office because of his relationship with a Wall Street financier who was under investigation.

Nixon already had one Supreme Court vacancy to fill before setting foot into the Oval Office. That was thanks to a Senate filibuster that had blocked the Democrats from replacing the chief justice in Johnson's final year in office. It was little different from the way the Republicans blocked Barack Obama's nominee to the Supreme Court in 2016.

After Fortas's departure, Nixon had two justice vacancies to fill at the start of his presidency. Two years after he filled those two slots, two more justices passed away, giving Nixon a total of four justices in his first term. One of those seats went to William Rehnquist. He was exactly the kind of right-wing ideologue who could roll back the 1960s and remake America as it used to be. One might say, "to make America great. Again." He had written a memo against desegregating schools and had been active in voter suppression in Arizona. He was on the Court for thirty-three years, including nineteen years as chief justice. One of his first big decisions was to vote against abortion rights in *Roe v. Wade.*

Nixon's fourth Supreme Court appointee was Lewis F. Powell, Jr., a specialist in corporate law and a board director of the Philip Morris tobacco group, which denied any link between smoking and cancer. The same year he was appointed to the Court, he wrote a memo that served as the blueprint for corporate America's power grab of the political system in Washington.

Powell was dismayed by the success of the activist Ralph Nader, who had the temerity to push the auto industry into saving the lives of its own customers. For a tobacco company board director, that was obviously a bizarre idea. Powell's memo, written for the US Chamber of Commerce, argued that everything from the New Deal to the 1960s had been a Communist attack on American free enterprise. Corporate America needed to step up and move the political needle against all that pernicious thought "from the college campus, the pulpit, the media, the intellectual and literary journals, the arts and sciences, and from politicians." In other words, everything Trump has tried to bully into silence in his second term.

Long before Republican states started to ban books from libraries, and long before Turning Point USA and the like showed up on high school and college campuses, Powell pushed for what he called "evaluation of textbooks" and "equal time on the college speaking circuit." He wanted the TV networks to be "monitored in the same way that textbooks should be kept under constant surveillance." He even wanted "well-written paperbacks or pamphlets on 'our side,'" as he called it.

Powell argued for a counterbalance of conservative think tanks and media to move public opinion. He especially wanted to allow corporate dollars to be treated like personal free speech. That was a political campaign he took into the Supreme Court, which eventually used his arguments to allow unlimited dark-money political contributions in the Citizens United case—because when you think about the original intent of the founding fathers, they obviously believed in the freedom of major corporations to spend ungodly sums of cash to manipulate our elections. "Business must learn the lesson, long ago learned by Labor and other self-interest groups," he wrote. "This is the lesson that political power is necessary; that such power must be assiduously cultivated; and that when necessary, it must be used aggressively and with determination—without embarrassment and without the reluctance which has been so characteristic of American business."

The memo was successful far beyond the fever dreams of the reactionary Right. It convinced the Chamber of Commerce to spend heavily to lobby the federal government. It led directly to wealthy conservatives funding think tanks and lobbying groups, magazines and media companies in order to push their pro-business, antigovernment agenda. It helped create the libertarian Cato Institute, the American Legislative Exchange Council to organize state officials, the Business Roundtable of CEOs, and the notorious Heritage Foundation. It was the Heritage Foundation that created a lengthy playbook for the incoming Reagan administration in 1981, stretching to twenty volumes and more than two thousand recommendations for how to shrink the federal government. That included stopping affirmative action to help women and minorities.

Somehow the military was not included in that right-wing vision for smaller government. Far from it; the foundation wanted Reagan to add tens of billions of dollars to the Pentagon budget every year to support anti-Communist forces around the world. That piece of warmongering advice led directly to the Iran-Contra scandal that almost sunk the Reagan presidency. Over the course of two Reagan terms, the Pentagon budget almost doubled to more than $320 billion, which in today's dollars is pretty much where it stands today, around $850 billion. Except that there's no Cold War playing out across a planet on the edge of nuclear annihilation. That didn't stop Trump from suggesting that the defense budget should balloon another half-trillion dollars in 2027.

The era of big government never ended. It just chipped away at the areas reformed by liberal America in the 1960s. One of Heritage's main funders was the billionaire Richard Mellon Scaife, the heir to the Mellon banking, oil, and aluminum fortune. (It's amazing how many free enterprise zealots inherited their cash piles, instead of creating them from scratch in their garage. Looking at you, David Ellison.)

Scaife pioneered the lie peddling that has become so familiar in the

Trump era through his newspaper, the Pittsburgh *Tribune-Review*. It was Scaife's paper that pushed the conspiracy theory that Bill and Hillary Clinton had been responsible for the death of their deputy White House counsel, Vince Foster. Among the writers who worked on that smear was Christopher Ruddy, who later founded Newsmax Media with the help of more Scaife dollars. Ruddy and Newsmax are such boosters of Donald Trump that the company ended up paying $67 million to settle a libel lawsuit for falsely claiming that Dominion Voting Systems had rigged the 2020 election results.

Which brings us to Project 2025, the crowning achievement of the Heritage Foundation's policy shop, with the worst possible outcomes for the American republic. If you're astonished at the rapid decline of our democracy, the sweeping illegality of Trump's actions, the rampant corruption and embrace of white nationalism, you can thank the Heritage Foundation for all that. Yes, it's true that Trump pretended he had nothing to do with it. "I know nothing about Project 2025," he wrote on Truth Social in July of election year 2024. "I have no idea who is behind it."

Was he lying, or was he truly clueless? Perhaps he was both, and perhaps it doesn't really matter—because the second coming of Trump bears a striking similarity to pretty much everything Project 2025 recommended. At the heart of the project was the overt politicization of federal government workers: the vetting of staff to determine their loyalty to the right-wing cause. That included the Justice Department, which had been protected from political influence since the days of Nixon's excesses. The Education Department would be dismantled; Medicare and Medicaid would be cut; tracking climate change would halt, along with its mitigation; diversity, equality, and inclusion (DEI) initiatives would end while the government pursued the concocted notion of antiwhite racism. Of course, the project included mass deportation of undocumented immigrants and the military being deployed on the streets of American cities.

"We are in the process of the second American Revolution," said Kevin Roberts, the head of the Heritage Foundation, on right-wing cable TV in July 2024. The project was never exactly modest or even really conservative. But Roberts did say that the revolution would "remain bloodless if the left allows it to be." Good to know the bullets would fly only if the Left provoked the revolutionaries to shoot.

Most of the authoritarian edicts detailed by the project were based on the previously fringe idea of "unitary executive power." In plain English, that means that the president runs the executive branch, something that everyone agrees is true. But what the far-right revolutionaries really mean is something much more expansive and autocratic. Instead of Congress and the courts working as the famous checks and balances of our republic, a president with full "unitary executive" power can fire anyone in an independent agency, including the prosecutors at the Justice Department and the governors of the Federal Reserve. A president can ignore laws or interpret them the way he likes and ignore the oversight of Congress. On anything to do with the military or foreign affairs, there is no need to consult with anyone, including on the decision to go to war. Trump would go so far as to say that his power was restrained only by his "own morality."

Here's the truth: The Republican embrace of a dictatorial president did not start with Donald Trump. Ronald Reagan expanded presidential power to fill government with his political friends. George W. Bush went further, in his so-called war on terror, by torturing detainees and imprisoning them indefinitely without charge or trial—all under the supposed powers of the unitary executive. They all paved the way for Donald Trump to become a version of the authoritarian leaders he has always admired around the world: if not a full-blown American Vladimir Putin or Kim Jong Un, then at least a pumped-up Viktor Orbán or Narendra Modi. "I have an Article II, where I have the right to do whatever I want as president," he said at the White House in 2019.

In fact, Article II of the Constitution simply says, "The executive Power shall be vested in a President of the United States of America." You can decide for yourself if that means a president can do whatever he wants. The same article says, for instance, that a president needs the "Advice and Consent of the Senate" to sign treaties and appoint ambassadors and other senior officials, as well as justices of the Supreme Court.

For its part, Trump's Supreme Court has decided to read that part of the Constitution differently from every other sane, impartial American. It ruled in the middle of the 2024 campaign that a president is immune to criminal prosecution for any official act, however that might be defined. The justices knew what was at stake. The case they were deciding, *Trump v. United States*, was about Trump's determined and entirely illegal attempts to reverse his defeat in the 2020 election. In other words, the strictly originalist judges—the ones who claim that they only interpret the Constitution precisely the way it was written—believe that the founding fathers wanted a kinglike president who could break the law with impunity, especially if it involves undermining the democratic process that reflects the will of the people.

It wasn't the first time the right-wing Court members had tipped the scales of justice in favor of their side. They had no problem handing the presidency to George W. Bush in December 2000, when the state of Florida had been deadlocked by a few hundred votes. Having argued again and again for states' rights, the conservative justices abandoned their supposed principles—as well as any commitment to democracy—by shoehorning the Republican candidate for president into office. When the highest court in Florida ordered a recount across the state that threatened Bush's supposed margin of victory of just 327 votes, the Supreme Court stepped in to stop the recount. They said it would cast a cloud over Bush's legitimacy to count the votes of the people, in line with the state's rulings. The conservatives made a special point of saying that their decision was "limited to the present circumstances." So it was both unprecedented and unprincipled.

It has taken the right wing several decades to reach that point. The complete reversal and retrenchment of the Democratic agenda for equal rights was intentional and organized, built on distortions and determination—but mostly on a Republican Party hell-bent on seizing power—and wielding it to its fullest extent.

There is nothing conservative about Project 2025; it has always been radical and revolutionary. It isn't about preserving freedoms; it is about root-and-branch reactionary response, ripping up the decades of social and economic progress made after the two world wars of the twentieth century. If it had been popular, the right-wing radicals would not have needed to seize power on the Supreme Court to protect their lawbreaking. They would not have needed to pretend that corporations were people, that the white majority was persecuted by antiracist policies, or that the Constitution was designed to give power to an American king.

Ernest Hemingway wrote that bankruptcy happens in two ways: "Gradually, then suddenly." That's how we're losing our democracy.

2

The Wrong Game

In so many ways, for so very long, Democrats have been following a playbook that is a half-century old. It was crafted by Bill Clinton, who led the Democrats out of the wilderness and back into the White House after twelve years of Republican rule under Reagan and Bush. Clinton was proudly and explicitly a moderate Democrat who could reach Republicans, an approach he liked to call the Third Way.

That meant he straddled both sides of the political divide on many issues. He supported the right of LGBT Americans to serve in the military but not openly, creating the bizarre policy called "Don't ask, don't tell." In case that was still too pro-LGBT, a few years later he signed the Defense of Marriage Act, which banned same-sex marriages. With the help of then senator Joe Biden, he got Congress to pass the Violent Crime and Law Enforcement Act of 1994 with a massive boost in funding to train new police officers and create new prisons. It introduced harsh mandatory minimum sentences and expanded the federal death penalty. At the same time, it banned assault weapons such as the AR-15 semiautomatic rifle and increased funding to protect women against domestic and sexual violence. Third Way politics pointed in all directions.

Clinton risked his first term on health care reform, crafting a complex patchwork of private and public insurance, led by First Lady Hillary Clinton. The plan managed to alienate everyone; liberals thought it was too small, conservatives claimed it was too big. That's the problem with trying to give something to everyone. The failure of Hillarycare led directly to the Republican revolution of the 1994 midterms, when Newt Gingrich's right-wing GOP took control of the House of Representatives for the first time since 1952. That disaster pushed Clinton to swing to the right and declare that the era of big government was over. He willingly signed welfare reform legislation that curtailed benefits and added work requirements—"Welfare to work," as it was called.

Surely—*surely*—all that trimming and hedging would win Clinton Republican support, right? The honest, objective answer was: Hell, no.

Clinton's biggest achievement was the Balanced Budget Act of 1993, which raised taxes and cut spending in an effort to deal with the budget-busting deficits left by Reagan and Bush throughout the 1980s. Coupled with the booming economy of the era, it worked. The federal budget moved into surplus for the first time since the 1960s. No chief executive has presided over anything close to a surplus since then.

For all the Republican blather about the deficit, you might think that Clinton had some support for his budget balancing. You'd be wrong. Not a single Republican voted for the 1993 legislation. Not one. In fact, far from rewarding Clinton's fiscal responsibility, they painted him as a tax-and-spend liberal in the elections that they swept the following year. They followed that by passing a House budget that slashed Medicare and cut taxes for the rich. They even shut down the government when Clinton said no to their inane scheme.

You could argue that the classic Clinton triangulation that followed the 1994 midterms managed to save his presidency, as he easily won reelection in 1996. That's true—up to a point. Clinton won, but the Democrats still failed to take back the House and Senate. So after all that centrism, in an era of peace and prosperity, Clinton won the White House and found himself with no power to pass any laws. Even worse, he was powerless to stop the endless torrent of investigations that eventually led the scandal-obsessed nation to his affair with Monica Lewinsky. Which naturally led to his impeachment. For all his charisma, his communication skills, and his calculated centrist appeals to all sides, Clinton failed to find any common ground with the Republican Party—at least anything its members would give him credit for.

The culmination of eight years of the great centrist president—the man who could embody and espouse the policies of the Left and Right—was the 2000 election. It wasn't exactly a resounding thumbs-up for centrist politics that could unite the nation; it was, instead, an election decided by a few hundred contested ballots in Florida and the jaw-dropping ruling of the right-wing Supreme Court.

* * *

Barack Obama embodied the same spirit of unity as Bill and Hillary Clinton despite their long and bitter rivalry in the 2008 primaries. If anything, he believed even more in his ability to unite a divided and fractured nation. As he famously said in his breakout speech at the 2004 Democratic convention, he believed that there was no red America or blue America, just the United States of America. With his personal and political skills, backed by a movement of inspired young volunteers and vote-switching independents, he honestly believed he could find common ground with the opposition.

On the eve of his inauguration, he hosted a dinner honoring the Republican nominee he had just easily beaten, John McCain. He praised him as an American hero and called for "a new way of doing the people's business in this city." In other words, he was staking everything on a bipartisan kumbaya, just like the dinner crowd he was talking to. "There are few Americans who understand this need for common purpose and common effort better than John McCain," he said.

Sure enough, his first order of business was to reach out to Republicans at the start of the Great Recession, triggered by the apocalyptic disaster that was the financial meltdown of 2008. Obama's $831 billion stimulus package included $275 billion in tax cuts, which the new president said the Republicans could shape. His reward for that outreach was not exactly what he had expected. The American Recovery and Reinvestment Act got precisely zero Republican votes in the House. In the Senate, it snagged three Republican votes. John McCain's was not among them.

This is what happened to Obama's earnest calls for bipartisanship at the start of a catastrophic economic crisis: the Tea Party. Two days after Obama signed the stimulus package into law, the right-wing "editor" Rick Santelli went live on CNBC from the floor of the Chicago Mercantile Exchange, where he ranted about the government "promoting bad behavior." He compared Obama's America to Cuba and talked about staging "a Chicago tea party." The traders around him whistled and cheered him on, and a ragtag protest movement was born.

The so-called Tea Party was quickly co-opted by the same corporate interests that funded the right-wing think tanks. It looked like a grassroots group, but it was in reality an AstroTurf operation, funded in large part by the Koch brothers, whose industrial conglomerate is one of the largest privately owned companies in the nation. David Koch was at the time the fourth richest person in America, and he sat on the board of the libertarian Cato Institute, which his brother had cofounded with two other men. The billionaire brothers, who had inherited their corporation and fortune from their father, created the shamelessly named group Citizens for a Sound Economy, which later splintered into Americans for Prosperity and FreedomWorks.

Their idea of prosperity and a sound economy did not include helping Americans out of the Great Recession. And it most definitely did not include helping Americans without medical insurance. Hiding behind the Tea Party, they opposed Obamacare at every turn, claiming that it was unconstitutional, socialist, and fatal for grandmas. The Tea Party helped Republicans take back the House in 2010. Its members soon ground politics to a halt and managed to shut down the government after two years in control of half of Congress.

Here's what really happened: The Affordable Care Act was modeled on Republican legislation in Massachusetts, led by the Republican governor, Mitt Romney, who would go on to be the party's nominee to attempt to unseat Obama in 2012. Republicans had no problem with Romneycare or Romney policies. Because their opposition was never about the policy; it was about power. Not a single Republican in the House voted for Obamacare. Not a single Republican in the Senate voted for Obamacare.

Republicans have tried to repeal Obamacare more than seventy times since it was passed. They came close in 2017, during Trump's first term, but they were thwarted by three Republicans. One of them, finally, was John McCain. Along the way, Republicans have found themselves on the wrong side of politics in their own country. When Obamacare was passed, 46 percent of Americans had a favorable view of it; today that number is 64 percent. That hasn't stopped the Republicans from slashing Obamacare subsidies. It turns out that there really are a red and a blue America. And they have no interest in being united.

That was always the plan: Obstruct and frustrate everything Obama represented. It started on the night of his inauguration, when Republican leaders met for dinner and pledged to oppose him at every step of the way. Less than two years later, the Senate Republican leader, Mitch McConnell, told the *National Journal* that there would never be any bipartisanship. "The single most important thing we want to achieve is for President Obama to be a one-term president," he declared.

* * *

One of the great fallacies of the Biden, Obama, and Clinton years is the notion that if only Democrats would compromise with their

Republican counterparts, their goodwill would be duly reciprocated. If only they capitulate to the GOP, this time—*this time*—the Right will lay down its arms and a golden era of bipartisanship would emerge. "I'll hold the ball," Lucy explains to Charlie Brown, "and you come running up and kick it."

When Republicans are in control, they wield power in a take-no-hostages manner. When Democrats are in control, they seek compromise, practice good governance, defend the institutions of government, and even make sacrifices to the minority in the hope that their selflessness, their righteousness, and their virtue will be rewarded. As was the case with Clinton, Obama, and Biden, they never are. Lucy isn't known for letting Charlie kick the football.

The political truth is this: Democrats like to signal their virtues, while Republicans like to swagger their virility. Democrats quaintly believe that being good is good enough to win elections. They think that Americans will admire them for standing up for civil rights and democracy, expanding health care, or saving the planet. They think that they can even win over Republican support by moving to the center and offering some juicy morsels of compromise. Republicans, on the other hand, think that Americans will admire them for looking strong, for wielding power, for extracting personal wealth from public well-being. Compromise is not part of their vocabulary.

Democrats love to tell themselves that good policy makes for good politics. They believe that they can unite the country by being smarter or more sincere than the other side. It's a messiah complex: Their nation-saving goodness will shine through their policies and become the popular success they surely deserve at the ballot box. Surely Republicans—at least the reasonable ones—will fall into line when they see how popular their perfectly moderated policies are?

Except that's not what happens. Every time.

Just before he lost the House to a Republican wave in 2010, Obama explained that he had been too busy to explain effectively what the Democrats were doing to save the economy. "We had to move so fast, we were in such emergency mode, that it was very difficult for us to spend a lot of time doing victory laps and advertising exactly what we were doing, because we had to move on to the next thing," he told a town hall in Seattle that October. ". . . We did not always think about making sure we were advertising properly what was going on."

But two years later, as his reelection campaign was gearing up, he was saying the same thing. "The mistake of my first term," he explained to CBS News, ". . . was thinking that this job was just about getting the policy right. And that's important. But the nature of this office is also to tell a story to the American people that gives them a sense of unity and purpose and optimism, especially during tough times." Now, this is from the Democratic president, whose communication skills are generational, historic, inspirational. His inner circle in his first term was full of seasoned messaging experts such as David Axelrod, Robert Gibbs, and Rahm Emanuel.

Well into his second term, Obama was still blaming his party's problems on its members' failure to sell their great works. This is how he analyzed the Republican sweep of Congress in the 2014 midterms, which paved the way for Trump's election two years later: "When you start governing, there is a tendency sometimes for me to start thinking *As long as I get the policy right, then that's what should matter,*" he told CBS News. ". . . I think that one thing that I do need to constantly remind myself and my team is it's not enough just to build the better mousetrap. People don't automatically come beating to your door. We've got to sell it. We've got to reach out to the other side and where possible persuade. And I think there are times, there's no doubt about it, where, you know, I think we have not been successful in going out there and letting people know what it is that we are trying to do and why this is the right direction."

People like to say that the definition of insanity is doing the same thing over and over again while expecting different results. How many times have you heard Democrats blaming their messaging skills, communication choices, or the other side's media advantages without taking a long, hard look in the mirror? Maybe, just maybe, the problem isn't the message or the advertising but the core belief that voters will reward good policy—or that they even value the kumbaya politics of national unity. That mindset is built on the notion that the majority of voters sit in the political center and will vote for leaders who govern like centrists, with more deference to the status quo than meaningful change.

That's not how politics works today. But it is how Democrats govern. An investigation into the failings of the Biden administration, compiled with the help of nearly four dozen former officials, found that those officials were hamstrung by their own inhibitions. They chose incremental policies due to "risk aversion" and were reluctant to pick "the fights worth having." Among those fights was one of the most basic values of the party: standing up for workers against corporate wrongdoing. Julie Su, the acting secretary of labor under Biden, told the Roosevelt Institute that her own department hadn't fully gone after corporations for offenses such as wage theft and weak safety protections. "What we needed was to meet that moment with boldness," she said. "There was too much hesitation." Instead, the administration was afraid of losing in court; afraid of publicity about their enforcement actions; afraid of politicizing corporations; afraid of alienating voters in the middle of a country that no longer had much of a political middle. They were, in essence, afraid of themselves.

It wasn't just the Labor Department; the Biden administration was afraid of "high-profile funding flops" even as it secured huge funding for green energy investments. Apparently one bad investment in the Obama years had been enough to inject so much fear and hesitation that it had slowed down the whole process. It's no coincidence that the bad investment in the solar panel maker Solyndra was one of the right-wing media's favorite "scandals" in the Obama years. To say it wouldn't register as a blip in the Trump era would be an insult to blips.

It's the same fearful attitude that led Attorney General Merrick Garland to wait a full year before announcing to the world that he intended to pursue anyone involved in the January 6, 2021, insurrection "whether they were present that day or were otherwise criminally responsible for the assault on our democracy." It took another three months for him to sign a memo approving the investigation into Trump. Even then, he was only bounced into moving things forward by the January 6th Committee hearings that summer. Garland then decided to wait until after the midterm elections in November to get started with the appointment of Special Counsel Jack Smith. In fact, he was so careful to avoid the accusation of a political witch hunt—and so fearful of upsetting Republicans—that he rejected three recommendations to expand the inquiry to include the man who had instigated the insurrection. Having wasted half his time in office, Merrick could only watch the clock run down as Trump gladly wasted the second half with legal delays.

It was typical of the Biden team, who tied themselves down in the pursuit of good government, relying too heavily on the bureaucratic process and measurements such as cost-benefit analyses. Their deep belief in good policy was well intentioned but totally self-defeating. They couldn't do enough because they were afraid of doing too much. They didn't want to pick fights in case someone picked a fight with them.

Democrats aren't stupid. They can read the same polls as Republicans do. They know what the voters want. The Biden team knew enough about the political pain of rising prices to call their landmark tax and spending package the Inflation Reduction Act of 2022. The law invested $783 billion in climate-friendly energy sources, as well as another $110 billion on Obamacare insurance subsidies. That was separate from the $1.2 trillion Infrastructure Investment and Jobs Act of November 2021. Which had nothing to do with the American Rescue Plan Act, which had pumped $1.9 trillion of stimulus into the covid-wrecked economy eight months earlier. All that spending dwarfed anything the Obama administration had managed to shovel out the door. But if you asked a hundred Democrats today to name the achievements of the Biden team, how many would name any one of those huge deals? You wouldn't need all the fingers on one hand to count them.

Was that a communication problem? Sure. But it's a symptom of the sickness, not the cause of it. Investing in the country's infrastructure and its transition to a green economy is obviously a good policy. But it is not great politics when the country is still struggling to emerge from the pandemic and its citizens are grappling with the cost of living and fearful of uncontrolled immigration.

Doing good isn't really good enough. It doesn't win over voters, who value change more than moderation. Yet time and again, that's how Democrats have positioned themselves: as the cleanup squad after another disastrous term of Republican rule. Bill Clinton was cleaning up the deficits after Reagan and George H. W. Bush. Barack Obama was cleaning up the wars and financial collapse after another Bush. Joe Biden was cleaning up the pandemic after the first Trump term. And the next Democratic president will be cleaning up after the corruption and autocracy of the second Trump term. But they won't get any credit for it, because the voters care about today and tomorrow, not yesterday or the next decade. They also won't get any credit because the cleanup will take so long.

They never do. Back in 2004, President George W. Bush was limping toward reelection as the war in Iraq turned into a quagmire of thousands of dead American soldiers and hundreds of thousands of dead Iraqi civilians. His Democratic opponent, Senator John Kerry, turned to former President Clinton for campaign advice. After all, Clinton had won two presidential elections, including one against Bush's father. He had left office with approval ratings in the mid-60s, even after his impeachment, so his political skills were clearly formidable. Kerry had been right about the disaster of the Vietnam War back in the early 1970s and felt he was right about the war in Iraq now. Clinton, however, had some blunt truths to deliver to Kerry, even as the polls suggested a close contest. "When people feel uncertain," he said, "they'd rather have somebody who is strong and wrong than someone who's weak and right."

Bush went on to win the popular vote by 2.4 percent—the largest margin of victory for a Republican president in the last forty years.

Over that same period, Republican presidents have won the popular vote only twice. For context, when Trump won in 2024, it was by a margin of only 1.5 percent. Strong and wrong beat weak and right.

Somehow when people talk about an evenly divided country, they are talking only about the times when Republicans win the White House. Joe Biden beat Donald Trump by 4.5 percent in 2020. Barack Obama won his first election by more than 7 percent in 2008 and his reelection by 3.9 percent.

In the aftermath of the 2024 election, in which Trump won the popular vote by 1.5 percent, I appeared on an episode of Piers Morgan's YouTube show *Uncensored*, where he said to me, "You've been all caught napping at the wheel. You fell asleep at the wheel and you let him drive by and take the whole shebang. I think Democrats should take a long, hard look in the mirror and admit you've just been completely pounded into total, shameful, humiliating oblivion. And you've gotta start again and you've gotta find politicians that actually resonate with the American people. And it's not the current shower you've got. Sorry." I asked him, "So Piers, in 2020, would you have said the same thing about the Republican Party that lost by a 4.5 percent margin nationally?" He replied simply: "No."

By any reasonable measure, the so-called populist Right isn't all that popular. Which poses the question: Why do Republicans run the White House as if they have a huge mandate to wield power, while Democrats run the White House with great concern about coalition building and signaling their virtues?

The Democrats who won reelection took a different tack: They muscled their way back to power by destroying their opponents. Was the Clinton economy humming in 1996, when it was time for his reelection? No. Was the Obama economy humming in 2012? Also no. Because they could hardly brag about the good times, both of them attacked their opponents early and often. Bob Dole was an old fool with a right-wing mob behind him. Mitt Romney was an out-of-touch corporate vulture with a right-wing mob behind him. Neither of them could understand the needs of working Americans.

Compare that to Joe Biden's reelection strategy. Donald Trump could have looked as old and befuddled as Bob Dole. He could have looked as weirdly rich as Mitt Romney. Instead, the billionaire who loves gold-painted mansions was a phony populist with some intuitive understanding of Americans living paycheck to paycheck.

Biden's pitch to the country before the 2022 midterms (which lost the House) was about what he called "the soul of the nation." Speaking in front of Independence Hall in Philadelphia, he practically hugged the founding documents of the nation and declared, "As I stand here tonight, equality and democracy are under assault. We do ourselves no favor to pretend otherwise." It was little different from the central argument of Kamala Harris's brief campaign.

They weren't wrong about Donald Trump and his MAGA mob; they were just wrong about the voters. Eight in ten voters, including 68 percent of Democrats, said that the economy was very important to them, according to the Pew Research Center. Health care came second at 65 percent of voters, ahead of crime and immigration. Gallup found that the economy was the only issue among twenty-two options that a majority of voters ranked as "extremely important." That was the highest since the Great Recession of 2008.

Democracy, the soul of the nation, healing a fractured nation: all good stuff, doing good for America, with good government and good people. The kind of stuff that moderates think will appeal to voters across the country. It was just all terrifically bad politics.

For his part, Barack Obama believes this is just a burden that Democrats must bear. "I think we have to acknowledge that we've got the harder job," he told me. "We believe in government as a tool for good, as a potential force to create more jobs, and as a way to make sure that the planet doesn't roast. To make sure that as we move forward, and the economy grows, that everybody—and not just some—are benefiting, and that kids are getting a good education. What that means is that we have to think about the consequences of our actions. We have to try to figure out how do we get working majorities to actually pass laws, and to implement those laws, and to make things happen. Tearing stuff down doesn't require that at all."

Still, even a great consensus-builder like Obama acknowledges that Democrats have been too quick to defend political institutions that should be treated as a means to an end—not an end in themselves. "I do think that there has been some unwillingness on the part of Democrats in the past to break down some of the institutional barriers for us getting stuff done just because, well, it's always been done that way," he told me. "I'll give you an example that frustrated the heck out of me when I was president, which was the filibuster in the Senate. The Senate is already structurally skewed and anti-majoritarian, right? It's hard for majorities to get stuff done, whether it's trying to pass civil rights legislation in the 60s or trying to get gun control legislation. Because even though majority people support it, Delaware and Wyoming have the same number of senators as California. That would require a constitutional amendment [to change]. You then compound that with a filibuster. And the truth is that Democrats for some time have been traditionalists in wanting to preserve that, when it blocks us from making government effective, which in turn makes people feel like government is corrupt and not caring about them. Which then gives folks like Trump an opening."

Still, even with a filibuster-free presidency, Obama would want Democrats to avoid copying Trump-style politics. "I don't want us to simply duplicate the behavior of the other side," he said. "I don't want us to have a slash-and-burn strategy where we don't care about rule of law. We don't care about some of the guardrails around our democracy. We start lying and having no regard for the truth, the way the other side seems to be comfortable with right now. Because if that's how we fight, then we lose what we're fighting for. But that doesn't mean we have to get punked or be saps, or cling to traditions just for the sake of tradition."

* * *

You don't need a thought experiment to understand how Republicans feel about political norms in the face of a crisis or disastrous poll numbers. Just look at what happened in the first two years of George W. Bush's presidency.

Bush took office after the contested election in 2000, which the right-wing Supreme Court shamelessly tipped in his favor. Instead of having his supporters storm the Capitol to protest the election result, his opponent, Al Gore, gave the most gracious concession speech imaginable. He quoted Abraham Lincoln's defeated rival, Senator Stephen A. Douglas, who had said, "Partisan feeling must yield to patriotism. I'm with you, Mr. President, and God bless you." While Gore said he strongly disagreed with the Supreme Court decision, he would not challenge it. "I accept the finality of this outcome," he declared. ". . . And tonight, for the sake of our unity as a people and the strength of our democracy, I offer my concession."

Sure enough, Democrats helped the newly elected Republican president out the gate. Bush spent the Clinton surplus on massive tax cuts, which twenty-eight Democrats voted for in the House and twelve Democrats voted for in the Senate. (Remember, not a single House Republican voted for Obama's stimulus package after he took office.)

That wasn't all. After his budget-busting tax cuts, Bush moved on to education reform. He didn't just receive Democratic support for his education bill; the whole thing was coauthored by the most effective Democratic senator in living memory, Ted Kennedy. Yes, the brother of JFK and RFK. It passed the Senate by eighty-seven votes. You could say that was way back when Republican presidents merely retooled the federal Department of Education rather than tried to abolish it. But the reality is that Democrats actually believed that their job was to find common ground in the name of national unity. How quaint.

Here's what happened after Al Qaeda terrorists struck on 9/11, on Bush's watch. Democrats rallied to support the sweeping Authorization for Use of Military Force, which passed the Senate with precisely zero votes against it. Only one House member voted against it: Barbara

Lee from Oakland, California, who rightly said that the legislation was a blank check for unlimited wars for all presidents. Since its passage, presidents have relied on that authorization to launch military ventures in dozens of countries. Two days after it became law, Bush addressed a joint session of Congress, warning the world, "Either you are with us, or you are with the terrorists."

At the time, nobody thought that would become the mantra for the Republican Party in its election campaigns moving forward. But a year later, during the 2002 midterm campaign, that was exactly what happened. Republicans didn't just wrap themselves in the flag. They suggested, very strongly, that Democrats were not with us but with the terrorists. In the Senate race in Georgia, Max Cleland was the sitting Democrat, a decorated Vietnam hero and triple amputee. His opponent, Saxby Chambliss (who had never served in Vietnam), ran TV ads pairing Cleland with Osama bin Laden and Saddam Hussein. The ads questioned his courage in keeping the homeland safe. Why was that? Because he wanted to give some union protections to the employees of the new Department of Homeland Security. John McCain, his fellow Vietnam veteran and friend, called the ads disgraceful and reprehensible. It didn't make any difference; Cleland was defeated by almost seven points, even though he had voted not just for Bush's tax cuts but also for the war in Iraq. It turned out that offering up all of that goodwill didn't exactly buy much.

That race was the first version of a Republican playbook that has become the party's entire political strategy.

It starts with the politics of fear. The enemy is everywhere, whether real or imagined. Of course, Al Qaeda's threat on 9/11 was real. But with every waterboarded confession from the prisoners at Guantánamo Bay came an endless stream of purported plans. There were many cells, many plots. Drones were going to attack the White House; blowtorches would melt the Brooklyn Bridge. There were Yemenis in Buffalo, Somalis in Columbus, Pakistanis in New York. If the terrorists weren't lurking everywhere, the soft, terrorist-loving Democrats certainly were.

The playbook continues with the politics of distraction. That didn't start with Trump's chaos. It started with Bush. In 2002, he had failed to finish the job against Al Qaeda and lost track of Osama bin Laden. Instead of pursuing public enemy number one, he switched his focus—and the world's—to Saddam Hussein in Iraq and his weapons of mass destruction, which I presume we'll discover around the same time as the Republicans' health care plan. If Bush had been serious about terrorism, he might have switched his focus to Iran, the biggest state sponsor of terrorism in the world, or even Saudi Arabia, home to fifteen of the nineteen 9/11 hijackers. But no. Both of those would have been too difficult. Iraq was supposed to be easy.

When it turned out to be anything but easy, it was time for the third part of the Republican game plan: the politics of personal destruction. You're either with us or with the terrorists. Never mind that it's an updated version of the slogan of the Italian Fascist leader Benito Mussolini; it works to polarize a nation, to simplify its choices, and to distort the democratic process while all the liberal traditionalists fret and worry about demagoguery.

Bush was limping toward his reelection in 2004 as the war in Iraq descended into the quagmire almost everyone had predicted. There were no weapons of mass destruction. Osama bin Laden was still on the run. The strong wartime leader looked like damaged goods.

That was when the Republicans reached for the Cleland strategy. The Democrats had nominated their own war veteran to run against Bush: Senator John Kerry, who had been decorated for his service in Vietnam, unlike Bush, who had never served. Kerry held a slender lead in the polls as he headed into his convention when a Republican group rolled out a series of ads that accused him of being a liar, a coward, and a traitor. The power of the ads was that they came from a group of Vietnam veterans who had served on a swift boat, just as Kerry had. They called themselves the Swift Boat Veterans for Truth, which sounded better than Swift Boat Veterans for Smears. They claimed that Kerry didn't deserve a Purple Heart, a Bronze Star, or a Silver Star. Fox News and the right-wing echo chamber happily peddled their lies, and Kerry's campaign struggled to respond. Kerry later told NPR that he had conceded to his staff, "If I heard that ad, I wouldn't vote for me." He never recovered his poll lead for any sustained stretch afterward.

The man behind the ads was Chris LaCivita, a political consultant and former marine who specializes in the politics of personal destruction. In the business, they call them attack ads. LaCivita tried to repeat the swift boat trick on Barack Obama, working on his supposed ties to the 1960s radical Bill Ayers. That was how vice presidential candidate Sarah Palin ended up saying that Obama "pals around with terrorists" in the closing weeks of the 2008 election. Obama, Osama—not much of a difference, is there?

LaCivita ended up as senior adviser and co–campaign manager on Trump's 2024 campaign, brought into the inner circle by Susie Wiles, who is now the White House chief of staff. He was also the chief strategist of the MAGA Inc. Super PAC, a supposedly independent group, as well as chief operating officer of the Republican National Committee. Far from backing away from the swift boat ads, he says, he'd "do it again tomorrow" if he could.

What kind of patriot is the man who questioned John Kerry's war medals? The kind of patriot who castigates a woman employed by Arlington National Cemetery, where the Trump campaign was photographing and shooting video in Section 60. That's the section where veterans of the Iraq and Afghanistan wars are buried. There are federal laws that prohibit the use of military facilities for political campaigns. LaCivita was part of a group that didn't just ignore the law or get into an altercation with a woman who was demanding respect for the law and the cemetery; he called her a "despicable individual" and posted the cemetery video on Twitter, hoping, as he put it, "to trigger the hacks" working for the secretary of the US Army. Insulting the army and disrespecting the nation's fallen troops: two tactics you don't often think are the hallmarks of someone dedicated to military valor and our national security.

* * *

Why are Democrats so far behind when it comes to playing this kind of politics? It may be distasteful, but it certainly works. Just look at the two times Democrats played hardball: during Clinton's reelection campaign in 1996 and Obama's reelection campaign in 2012. Their campaign staff worked hard to diminish their opponents, and they both sailed to victory. However, in normal times, Democrats are too busy believing their own myths about their ability to unify a fractured nation with good policies and good government. Surely that must lead to good poll numbers, right?

Once in the White House, Team Obama did not spend a whole lot of time blaming the Great Recession on Republicans for relaxing financial regulation to the point where nobody knew what risks they were playing with. At the very start of his first term, Obama had attacked Wall Street bankers—not Republican deregulation—for what he called "the height of irresponsibility" for paying themselves huge bonuses after receiving emergency bailouts from taxpayers. If you think "the height of irresponsibility" would barely count as fightin' words, you'd be wrong. The backlash from Wall Street was deep and enduring, as the banks threw their support behind his Republican rival in 2012. "It's personal," explained *Wall Street Journal* reporter Gregory Zuckerman. "They feel insulted by President Obama."

It wasn't just the financial crisis that dodged real accountability; the same was true for the darkest corners of Bush's war on terror, especially the use of torture on detainees. Obama released the legal memos that approved torture by CIA operatives but opposed the prosecution of those responsible. He even opposed an independent inquiry. "Nothing will be gained by spending our time and energy laying blame for the past," he said in April 2009, using language that has never crossed the mind or lips of Donald Trump. Even well into Obama's second term, he admitted that "we tortured some folks" but said we needed to understand what the CIA had been going through at the time, so we should not "feel too sanctimonious" about the torture.

At least Obama could put an end to Bush's torture and war. Joe Biden had less luck putting an end to Trump's botched handling of the covid pandemic. During the election of 2020, Biden said that Trump's approach had been to wave "the white flag." He was responding to Bob Woodward's reporting that Trump had wanted to "play it down" while the pandemic spread. "He walked away," Biden told CNN. "He didn't do a damn thing. Think about it. . . . it's almost criminal."

Given that Trump's behavior had been almost criminal, did Biden spend his first year blaming Trump for the United States' having a worse fatality rate than Italy, Germany, and France? Not exactly. Instead, as Republican governors resisted Biden's vaccination and mask policies, Biden effectively said that there was little he could do. Vaccine mandates were a decision for local governments, school districts, and companies to make, he explained. "My guess is, if we don't start to make more progress, a lot of businesses and a lot of enterprises are going to require proof for you to be able to participate," he told reporters at a news conference in the summer of 2021.

If you're wondering how the vaccine deniers managed to spread their lies and conspiracies so far and wide under Trump, you could look at Biden's response to the vaccine deniers when he took office. By avoiding a fight with MAGA Republicans, he allowed the spread of another virus: the disease of antiscientific ignorance that will harm the public health for generations. He didn't force governors to follow the science by denying their states federal funds. He didn't force corporations to follow the science by threatening to end federal contracts. He didn't blame Republicans for effectively killing thousands of Americans, for failing to keep the country safe from harm.

Long before we reached the 2024 election, strong and wrong was already beating weak and right. You could say that demonizing the opposition is bad for the country. But you can't say it's worse than Donald Trump's presidency. The cold, hard truth is that Republicans have been playing the long game, while Democrats have been playing the wrong game.

3

Blank Checks and Balances

Five months into Trump's crazy reign over the nation's capital, a single Senate staffer stood in the way of the monstrous tax-cutting bill that was branded as big and beautiful. Elizabeth MacDonough started her career working in the Senate library before moving on to become an editor for the *Congressional Record*. She worked for the Justice Department and then joined an obscure team that advises Senate leaders on the institution's rules and precedents: the Senate parliamentarian's office. In 2012, she became only the sixth Senate parliamentarian since the role was established in 1935, when the flood of New Deal legislation threatened to overwhelm the poor confused senators. "No matter who is in my office asking for assistance, I represent the Senate with its traditions of unfettered debate, protection of minority rights, and equal power among the states," MacDonough told students at Vermont Law School in 2018. In other words, she represents the democratic norms and traditions that Donald Trump and his henchmen have delighted in trashing since they took office.

MacDonough's power lies in her referee role on the use of the filibuster—or, more precisely, her power to decide what legislation can dodge the filibuster rules that require sixty votes to end debate and move to a Senate vote. You see, there are various carve-outs for the precious filibuster. The biggest of these is bills relating to the budget, which defines how the federal government taxes and spends our money. We live in an era when Republicans think they were put on the planet to cut their own taxes. So the budget carve-out for the filibuster covers most of what constitutes a Republican sweet spot.

As they bulldozed their way into colossal budget deficits, Trump's Republicans wanted to slash Medicaid funding while also somehow protecting health care for those at the bottom of the economic ladder. That meant forcing the states to fill the funding hole they had just created. MacDonough ruled that the Medicaid ruse was out of bounds, not a legitimate part of a budget bill.

Oklahoma Senator (later named Secretary of Homeland Security) Markwayne Mullin, a former cage fighter who believes that the 2020 election was stolen, said she seemed "politically motivated." Alabama Senator Tommy Tuberville, a former football coach who thinks that Trump could serve an unconstitutional third term, posted that she "SHOULD BE FIRED ASAP." Other Trump loyalists hedged their positions by not ruling the question out or in. Senator Lindsey Graham of South Carolina said he had "no intention" of sidestepping her, while Senator Josh Hawley of Missouri said he "just can't imagine" how they would get the votes to do so.

As for Trump himself, he refused to say whether anyone should respect her decisions. "The parliamentarian has been a little difficult," he said. "And I would say that I disagree with the parliamentarian on some things and on other ways she's been fine. But we'll have to see." Two days later, he was enthusiastically backing calls from House MAGA hard-liners to ignore her. "An unelected Senate Staffer (Parliamentarian), should not be allowed to hurt the Republicans [*sic*] Bill," he posted. "Wants many fantastic things out. NO!"

That's not how any of this works. Yes, MacDonough was appointed by Democratic former Senate majority leader Harry Reid. But she ruled against the Democrats back in 2021, when they wanted to increase the minimum wage in a covid relief bill. The difference between now and then? The Biden White House didn't rage against a Senate staffer for the crime of doing her job. "President Biden is disappointed in this outcome," said press secretary Jen Psaki. "He respects the parliamentarian's decision and the Senate's process." It took Bernie Sanders, the Senate Budget Committee chairman at the time, to point out the inconsistency of that decision. Just four years earlier, MacDonough had said it was fine to include drilling for oil in the Arctic National Wildlife Refuge in the Trump tax cuts of 2017. Naturally, Trump had nothing to say about the parliamentarian when she was ruling in his favor. The norms of democracy are apparently worth upholding only when the outcome is good for Donald Trump.

It's actually not unprecedented to fire the parliamentarian. Republicans last booted one out in 2001 because they were frustrated about what they claimed were "inconsistent calls" that "made it hard for the leadership to plot a strategy," as one staffer told *The New York Times*. That firing was not forgotten by Trump's fan base on Capitol Hill.

The US Senate likes to call itself the greatest deliberative body in the world. But that modest claim is not based on the words of the Constitution; it's a cultural state of mind, a collection of rules and expectations that can—and have—changed over time. It relies on respect for tradition, on the wisdom drawn from lessons learned, on the notion that institutions are credible. In other words, it relies on nothing that Donald Trump values and nothing the courts can hold on to.

Let's remember why Richard Nixon quit the presidency after the Watergate scandal led right to his Oval Office. He did not lose his impeachment trial in the Senate. In fact, he didn't even stand trial, unlike Donald Trump, who faced two impeachment trials. Nixon resigned without even being impeached in the House. All it took was the opening of an impeachment inquiry to push him out. The terms of that inquiry look quaint today. There was Nixon's obstruction of justice to stop the criminal investigation into the Watergate break-in—namely, his political manipulation of the Justice Department. There was his abuse of power by using the FBI and IRS to investigate his opponents. And there was his contempt of Congress for refusing to comply with its investigations. In other words, a regular Tuesday in Trump's Washington.

Nixon wanted to tough it out, to stand trial. But he was bleeding support from his own Republicans in Congress because his credibility was shot to pieces. And so he became the only US president in history to resign—and the only one to leave power through the impeachment process—because he lost both his credibility and the nation's trust.

There was a sense, widely believed and now entirely lost, that a president's character was key to whether he should hold power and whether American democracy could endure. Those days are long gone. You could try to glue the eggshell back together, but the system of checks and balances that pushed Nixon out of power is broken. What's left are obscure Senate rule makers who can be fired without anyone understanding what they do or why.

* * *

Don't get it twisted. Donald Trump could not dismantle democracy on his own; he needs the obedience of an almost entirely spineless Congress to rip up the Constitution. And its members have happily obliged, no matter how much humiliation he heaps upon them.

The founders of our democratic republic made it crystal clear where power should reside. They did not start the Constitution with the presidency. Article I, Section 1, is about Congress, stating specifically and clearly that "all legislative Powers" rest in the Senate and House. Section 8 defines those powers more clearly: "To lay and collect Taxes, Duties, Imposts and Excises . . . To regulate Commerce with foreign Nations . . . To establish a uniform Rule of Naturalization. . . . To promote the Progress of Science and useful Arts . . . to define and punish Piracies and Felonies committed on the high Seas . . . To declare War."

You get the picture: the power to set the federal budget; the power to impose tariffs; the power to decide who should be a citizen; the power to abolish organizations supporting science and the arts; the power to blow up ships off the coast of Venezuela; the power to bomb Iran. None of these powers rests with the presidency or Donald Trump—unless the Congress has decided to contract every ounce of its autonomy to another coequal branch of government.

That was not a scenario the founders imagined, as they strongly believed that human nature would never willingly surrender power. I guess they weren't quite capable of grasping the servility of Mike Johnson.

Then again, they also believed that a president should be removed from office for "Treason, Bribery, or other high Crimes and Misdemeanors." And that nobody in any office should "without the Consent of the Congress, accept of any present, Emolument, Office, or Title, of any kind whatever, from any King, Prince, or foreign State."

You don't need a Harvard law degree or a Supreme Court clerkship to know that would absolutely prohibit a president from accepting a Boeing 747 luxury jetliner as a gift from the emir of Qatar—especially if that plane was going to be the personal property of the same president after he left office. Not without the Consent of the Congress, of course.

Even though the idea of cryptocurrency assets would have been unthinkable in 1776, the founders would surely have recognized the threat to the republic from the $802 million the Trump Organization raked in during just the first half of the first year of Trump's second term—especially because all those hundreds of millions of dollars were propped up by sales of World Liberty tokens, including a $100 million purchase by an obscure company called Aqual Foundation, based in the United Arab Emirates. The man behind Aqual is a Chinese businessman named Guren "Bobby" Zhou, who is under investigation in the United Kingdom for money laundering.

If you think that sounds like another crypto scandal, you're not wrong. Trump granted a pardon to Changpeng Zhao, the founder of the Binance crypto exchange, who pleaded guilty to money laundering in 2023. Binance just happened to strike a deal with World Liberty Financial, involving a $2 billion business transaction by the UAE-backed firm MGX. The deal was announced in Dubai by Zach Witkoff, the founder of World Liberty Financial, who also happens to be the son of Steve Witkoff, Trump's envoy to the Middle East. To call these deals a conflict of interest is like calling the asteroid that killed the dinosaurs a thunderstorm.

What does it say about this Republican-led House that there's such a deafening silence about the colossal buck raking by the Trump family? How can anyone reconcile it with the nearly three-hundred-page report issued by the House Oversight Committee's special investigation into the Biden family's business activities?

For context, this gang of House Republicans opened a formal impeachment inquiry into Joe Biden because his son, Hunter, was consultant to the Ukrainian energy company Burisma. At its most scandalous and scurrilous, there were unproven allegations about Russian wires for $3.5 million or loan repayment checks for $200,000. The committee chairman, James Comer, alongside Senator Chuck Grassley, wrote to the then Attorney General Merrick Garland and FBI Director Christopher Wray, saying that a whistleblower had revealed that policy decisions were being made in exchange for foreign cash. Shocking, if true. Of course, it wasn't. The whistleblower was a former FBI informant, Alexander Smirnov, who pleaded guilty to lying to the FBI about the Burisma bribery story. His lies had been based on instructions from Russian intelligence officials.

There's that Russian hoax again. It did not lead to Biden's impeachment, but it did lead to years of screeching headlines on Fox News and the rest of the right-wing echo chamber—which, of course, was the goal; not the facts but the narrative.

In May 2023, midway through his pretend investigation, Comer told Fox News that Trump's polling lead over Biden was due to his dirty work: "I believe that the media is looking around, scratching their head, and they're realizing that the American people are keeping up with our investigation."

It should come as no surprise to the House Oversight Committee, but the idea of oversight is "to ensure . . . the accountability of the federal government and all its agencies." It's to "provide a check and balance on the role and power of Washington." It's to "expose waste, fraud, and abuse." That shouldn't be a surprise, because those fine words come from the web page explaining the mission of the House Oversight Committee, under a smiling photo of one James Comer.

What may be surprising is that, a year after Trump's reelection, Comer had dumbed down the idea of checks and balances to this: a report on Biden's use of autopen signatures. That wasn't long after he wrapped up a hearing on how Congress "must build on President Trump's success in combating crime in the nation's capital."

This Congress isn't toothless. It's gumless.

* * *

The heart of the power of Congress is supposed to be its control over the budget. Presidents traditionally propose budgets, but members of Congress are the ones who set the actual numbers. This is not a small detail buried in an obscure corner of the Constitution; it's central to the notion of coequal branches of government.

You may have heard how the founders felt about taxation without representation. They did not appreciate the notion that a king could set his own budget without regard to the wishes of the people, as expressed by their democratically chosen representatives. That's why the Constitution says that tax bills need to start in the House, the body that was supposed to be closest to the people, with direct elections for every member every two years. That's why the most powerful committee on the Hill has traditionally been the House Ways and Means Committee, which is supposed to manage taxes and tariffs. It's why there's normally a scramble to get a seat on the appropriations committees that fund the government's activities.

Those days are over; the roles, reversed. Congress may pass a spending bill here or there. It may negotiate some complex horse-trading deal between the parties to reach the number of votes it needs to pass a bill. It may fund agencies and departments established by laws passed by previous Congresses. However, all of it—or any of it—can be ignored or even rescinded by the president, as long as Congress rolls over and plays dead.

Washington wonks call them rescissions, which means the cancellation of an agreement. Presidents have been required to follow a special process of rescissions since the post-Nixon reforms of 1974. Congress at that time believed that Nixon was abusing his power by withholding funds for programs he didn't like—whether for medical research, public housing, or education. They thought it was an obvious and unconstitutional way for a president to avoid complying with the laws they passed. Sure enough, conservative lawyers agreed with Congress. Among them, two went on to become chief justices of the Supreme Court: William Rehnquist and John Roberts. "No area seems more clearly the province of Congress than the power of the purse," Roberts wrote when he was a young lawyer in the Reagan White House.

So where does that power lie now? In his first year back in the White House, Trump asked to rescind $9.4 billion of congressionally ordered spending, mostly on foreign aid and public media funding. This spineless Congress handed him back $9 billion. In contrast, Biden, Obama, and Bush rescinded precisely zero dollars. In fact, when Trump asked for $42 billion of rescissions in his first term, Congress granted him absolutely zip.

Now, you could say that $9 billion is the federal equivalent of a pocket full of coins in a budget that totals $6.8 trillion. But rescissions are not the only way this Trump White House has stolen budget power from a self-castrated Congress. From the moment Elon Musk and his team of tech fanboys stormed federal government offices, Trump has ignored congressional budgets and federal laws, daring the courts to slow down or stop him.

Take the Consumer Financial Protection Bureau, established by law in 2010, after the financial meltdown, to tackle fraud by banks, credit card companies, payday lenders, and debt collectors. It's technically an independent section of the very independent Federal Reserve. Republicans have always hated it because their friends and donors in the financial sector don't want to be regulated by an agency that has returned more than $21 billion to the consumers they ripped off. Rather than abolish the agency, which would take the passage of an actual law in Congress, the Trump White House just decided to ignore the law—and Congress—altogether. Russell Vought, the architect of Project 2025 who now runs the Office of Management and Budget, told all CFPB staff to stop work less than two weeks after Trump was sworn into office. He closed the DC headquarters of the agency, shut down its website and social media accounts, and cut 90 percent of its staff.

Let's be clear: It's not just abnormal for Trump to seize power over the budget, it's illegal. It's unconstitutional. It can happen only because his own MAGA Republicans in Congress don't have the backbone to stand up for themselves or the law. They have no identity and purpose beyond pleasing Donald Trump. But there are consequences to this type of Pavlovian politics. There is no point in negotiating an agreement with a pack of obedient dogs if the top dog is going to piss all over the deal. So why should the Democrats take anything at face value—any promises, any handshakes, any commitments—from their Republican counterparts in Congress? What budget are they actually negotiating and voting for if that budget can be ignored, at will, by this White House?

On the face of it, the government shutdown of 2025 was about medical insurance subsidies. But in reality it was triggered by Trump's unconstitutional grab of the power of the purse.

There can be no trust when there is no respect for the law. And when there's no respect for the law, there's no respect for Congress. There was a time, not so long ago, when administration officials would sit patiently in front of congressional committees and endure their members' interrogations with polite responses. The reason was that Congress could mess with their budgets. Even if they objected to the line of questioning, they never wanted to risk a fight over their own funding.

Not anymore. When Pam Bondi, the then-attorney general of the United States, was asked about the lobbying activities of her former law firm, she decided that her best course of action was to insult the Democratic senator asking the question, Richard Blumenthal of Connecticut. Blumenthal, a former state attorney general, asked if Bondi had had any conversations with her former law firm as her department had reviewed a recent merger. Bondi's respect for Congress was clear. "Senator Blumenthal, I cannot believe that you would accuse me of impropriety when you lied about your military service," she said. "You lied. You admitted you lied to be elected a US senator. How dare you? I'm a career prosecutor. Don't you ever challenge my integrity. Do not question my ability to be fair and impartial as attorney general."

Bondi isn't the only law enforcement official who apparently couldn't care less about respecting Congress. When Senator Adam Schiff of California asked FBI Director Kash Patel about the Jeffrey Epstein files, Patel's response bordered on the unhinged. "We have countlessly proven you to be a liar in Russiagate, in January 6," he said. "You are the biggest fraud to ever sit in the United States Senate. You are a disgrace to this institution and an utter coward. I'm not surprised that you continue to lie from your perch and put on a show so you can go raise money for your charade. You are a political buffoon at best."

Liars, frauds, disgraces, buffoons. You would be hard pressed to find a single time when any official from any previous administration—Democratic or Republican—hurled such insults at members of Congress. They do so now with impunity and without shame because they know that there will be no consequences. Congress has surrendered its power of the purse. It has no say in authorizing military action. It is uninterested in being a coequal branch of government. It stinks of fear, weakness, and self-loathing.

* * *

These aren't just blips or small, subtle breaks with the norm. You don't get to destroy the concept of checks and balances for four years, then return to the old ways. That's not how power works. The system has changed because the relationship between Congress and the White House has changed. It's a little ironic that the MAGA gang picked a fight with the Senate parliamentarian—because they have shifted our system of government to something that looks a lot like a parliamentary one.

With a parliament, the executive branch runs the legislature. The head of government—a prime minister, normally—is also the leader of the lawmakers. He or she has a seat in Parliament, merging the two branches of government. This is the system in Great Britain and Canada, Japan, and Germany. There are also heads of state—kings, queens, presidents—but they are ceremonial figures.

The system is essentially an elected monarchy. The British prime minister acts in the name of "the Crown" with the unrestricted powers of the monarch, as long as he or she controls the majority of the Parliament. Its members pass the budgets they want, when they want them. If they cannot pass those budgets, the government falls. There are committees and hearings, but they are toothless. There may be debates and televised question sessions, but they're performative. There's a vast difference between yelling insults at a prime minister and issuing subpoenas to investigate wrongdoing. The only real check and balance on executive power is a general election, when the voters get the chance to kick them out of power—or let them rule for another term.

In Trump's Washington, does anybody doubt that the person running the legislature is Donald Trump? He is the president and prime minister wrapped up in one.

In a parliamentary system, the minority has no power. The majority rules. Members of Parliament can occasionally buck their own prime minister. They can tweak legislation or force a leadership contest. They can also look like a pale imitation of democracy, like the Russian Duma, the lower house of the Federal Assembly, established after the collapse of the Soviet Union in 1993. In its first decade, the Duma included a mix of parties and power blocs. Initially, the parties supporting Boris Yeltsin, the country's first post-Soviet president, did not have complete control; they relied on right-wing nationalists for power. Then the old Communists won a majority in the Duma. In its second decade, Vladimir Putin's party, United Russia, took control and never looked back. The Duma was never given much power in the 1993 constitution. It has even less power under Putin, serving as the rubber stamp for a supposedly elected dictator.

We have not yet reached the rubber-stamp phase in the United States. But we are closer to a parliamentary system than to the congressional model that dominated the last century of our politics. In a parliament, there is no notion of bipartisanship, no value placed on agreement across the aisle. There's a majority, and that's where the power lies.

If Democrats learn anything from the Trump years—if they want to defend democracy and ensure that it will survive for another 250 years—they need to understand, accept, and exploit that shift in how Congress works. Because the old norms aren't coming back. Republicans aren't suddenly going to respect them, even if they complain when they're in the minority.

Democrats need to get comfortable with exercising the power of the majority in Congress. Or else get comfortable watching as power is wielded against them for a lifetime. They don't need to insult senators to their face. They don't need to ignore the oversight or budget powers of Congress. But they do need to realize that the days of bipartisan independence have long gone.

* * *

The very notion of bipartisan politics is based on a political culture that died out in the 1990s, a full generation ago—and a full generation after the parties began to realign along ideological lines. The trigger for this national upheaval was, as usual in American politics, race. Once the Democrats embraced the civil rights movement, there was little room for conservative southern Democrats to hang on to their Civil War–era loyalties. Once Republicans became the party of southern segregationists, there was little room for liberal northern Republicans. The first president to manipulate this was Richard Nixon, with his notorious southern strategy, which played on racist politics to realign pro-segregation voters against the Democrats. Some remnants of the old party alignments have lingered on: a Democratic senator in West Virginia, a Republican senator in Maine. They are endangered species whose political life expectancy is already over.

Bipartisanship was a fact of life when both parties contained both liberals and conservatives. Creating cross-party coalitions was how business was done in Washington. Today, bipartisanship means finding a tiny number of votes from the other side so you can pretend that there's a broad base of support for your policies. It's a noble effort that belongs to another era. The only mechanism that is propping up this pretense is the filibuster, a tool to force bipartisan votes or—far more often—to grind Congress to a standstill.

You could argue that bipartisanship helps forge some national unity in a large and fractured country. But in reality, there is no higher purpose, no patriotic inspiration, that comes from a deadlocked Congress. The filibuster just deepens the distrust in our elected officials; people feel that they talk forever and do nothing to solve the mountain of problems we face. So we find ourselves in the ludicrous situation where Congress has nullified the filibuster on what it considers essential business, such as the budget. But it still pretends that the filibuster is all that protects us from tyranny. Remember: The filibuster is not part of the Constitution, a document written by people who *were* keenly attuned to the dangers of tyrants and feckless parliaments.

The filibuster does not exist for budget bills, because taxation and spending are too important to block. It does not exist for international trade deals or the authorization of military action—because, of course, global affairs are too important to filibuster. It does not exist if Congress wants to repeal laws passed by the District of Columbia, because Republicans can't stand having a real democracy in their backyard. It has been suspended to raise the debt limit, because a debt default was too important to risk in 2021.

In 2005, Republicans tried and failed to end the filibuster for judicial appointments. Eight years later, Democrats ended the filibuster for executive and judicial appointments except for the Supreme Court. Four years after that, Republicans ended the filibuster for the Supreme Court so that Trump could force through his right-wing nominee Neil Gorsuch.

This is where we ended up: Republican priorities such as taxes and stacking the courts with right-wing ideologues can pass with a simple majority vote; Democratic priorities such as gun control, saving the planet, immigration reform, abortion rights, and protecting democracy—they need sixty votes or else they can't move forward.

Even with the deck stacked in their favor, the Trump toadies want more. It didn't take a year in office for Trump to try to demolish the filibuster as one of the very few constraints on his power. In the middle of the long government shutdown in late 2025, he finally woke up to the fact that the roadblock to his spending bills was the filibuster. When some of his own Republican senators rebuffed his calls to eliminate the filibuster, other MAGA mobsters were more than ready to take up the fight. One of the MAGA challengers to a sitting senator, Wesley Hunt of Texas, attacked Senator John Cornyn for defending the filibuster. His fellow primary challenger Ken Paxton agreed with Trump that the filibuster should go. In South Carolina, Paul Dans, the primary challenger of Senator Lindsey Graham, said that "the filibuster is the last refuge of the RINO"—Republicans In Name Only. Challengers in Georgia and Kentucky did the same to sitting Republican senators in their states.

There is some rare consensus across the aisle, because even the most loyal Democratic defenders of the Senate's traditions know that the filibuster is a bust. There are few people alive who believe in the Senate more than Joe Biden, who served as Delaware's senator for thirty-six years and is considered the ultimate institutionalist. But in his first year as president, he said he was open to ending the filibuster to pass voting rights legislation that Republicans were blocking. The Freedom to Vote Act was supposed to end partisan gerrymandering, protect early voting, allow for automatic voter registration and same-day voter registration, curb secret dark-money donations, and end the long voting lines that somehow always happen to plague predominantly Black and Latino neighborhoods. Above all, it was a response to Trump's efforts to overturn the 2020 election, which he lost, by protecting local election officials, stopping people from tampering with election results, and allowing voters to sue if officials fail to certify election results.

Even Joe Biden thought that the filibuster was worth ending to protect democracy. "We're going to have to move to the point where we fundamentally alter the filibuster," he told a CNN town hall. Voting rights, he said, were just as important as raising the debt limit. However, he also said that they weren't as important as his big spending bills. Eliminating the filibuster would mean the end of his economic plans, he claimed.

At the same time, there were two archdefenders of the filibuster among Democratic senators: Joe Manchin of West Virginia and Kyrsten Sinema of Arizona, both of whom insisted that the filibuster was the biggest safeguard of bipartisanship and the great protector against extremism—as if they had never seen a Trump presidency and couldn't imagine what a second one might unleash on the people who had elected them to the Senate in the first place.

So the filibuster stayed, and voting rights died.

We have a clear choice if we want to restore our democracy. We need to end the filibuster and the notion that it protects both parties equally. It doesn't. It protects a status quo that the voters have rejected time and time again. It's worth remembering that our elected officials are in office to serve the people, not the institutions and processes of government. The institutions are not an end; they're a means to an end.

4

The Untouchables

Renee Good had just dropped off her son at school in Minneapolis and was on her way home when she chanced upon a cluster of Trump's secret police. Some of the neighbors were standing guard because those armed and masked ICE immigration officers were hanging around a bilingual elementary school nearby. Good wasn't an activist or a serial protestor. There was nothing in her past or present that qualified her as a "domestic terrorist," as Secretary of Homeland Security Kristi Noem called her. She was a mom of three, a poet and writer; a US citizen observing law enforcement officers on public streets. She was posing a threat to nobody when an ICE agent, along with Renee's wife, told her to drive away in her SUV. Another agent tried to open her door, and she began to drive away. That was the moment when ICE agent Jonathan Ross fired three shots at close range and murdered her.

ICE's presence in Minneapolis was the culmination of deployments across the country, beginning in my city of Los Angeles in the summer of 2025. The secret police staged hundreds of raids across the city in areas where Latinos work, shop, and live. At car washes and in parking lots, at food trucks and in supermarkets, masked officers violently detained anyone who looked suspiciously Latino. The raids came just a few weeks after Trump posted on Truth Social that he wanted to "liberate Los Angeles from the Migrant Invasion." At the same time, his deputy chief of staff, Stephen Miller, told Fox News that the White House had ordered its officers to make at least three thousand arrests a day.

The American Civil Liberties Union promptly filed a lawsuit based on the fundamental protections of the Bill of Rights. Specifically, the Fourth Amendment gives us all protection against unreasonable searches and seizures by the government. That's why police need a warrant to bust into your home. That's why they need to show probable cause to obtain a warrant from a judge. And if you're not at home, if you're walking down the street, that's why they need to argue that you were doing something suspicious. It's a low bar, for sure. But a suspicious officer is obliged to stop and ask questions to see if there are grounds to be suspicious. They can't just lock you up for your looks. Not legally, anyway. Which is to say, a racist police officer cannot claim that you look suspicious simply because of the color of your skin, because for years the courts have said that race is not enough for an officer to feel suspicious. Until now.

The ACLU's lawsuit quoted Stephen Miller as saying that the officers need not investigate their targets ahead of a raid; they should just go out and round people up. It stated:

> This comprehensive scheme has been guised as a crackdown on the "worst of the worst." But the preponderance of individuals stopped and arrested in the raids have not been targeted in any meaningful sense of the word at all, except on the basis of their skin color and occupation. Those who have borne the brunt of Defendants' heavy-handed pattern of unlawful conduct include day laborers, car wash workers, farm workers, street vendors, service workers, caregivers and others who form the lifeblood of communities across Southern California. Over a thousand res-

idents in the District have already been impacted, including a shocking (though hardly surprising) number of US citizens and individuals lawfully present in the country.

Nine days after the lawsuit was filed, a federal judge issued a temporary restraining order on the immigration raids. In doing so, Judge Maame Frimpong asked and answered a couple of simple questions. "Do all individuals—regardless of immigration status—share in the rights guaranteed by the fourth and fifth amendments to the Constitution? Yes, they do," she wrote. "Is it illegal to conduct roving patrols which identify people based upon race alone, aggressively question them, and then detain them without a warrant, without their consent, and without reasonable suspicion that they are without status? Yes, it is."

Three weeks later, the appeals court in Southern California upheld the temporary restraining order. Trump's lawyers promptly took the case to the Supreme Court. A month later, the Supremes released their decision. There was no hearing to explore the case, no questioning of the lawyers involved. There was no explanation of the majority decision, which was apparently 6–3—along ideological lines, of course. We can't be sure because there was no majority opinion provided. It was all part of what's called the shadow docket or emergency docket, where the Supreme Court has ushered through Trump's illegality under the cover of darkness.

There was, however, this laughable concurring opinion from Justice Brett Kavanaugh:

The Government sometimes makes brief investigative stops to check the immigration status of those who gather in locations where people are hired for day jobs; who work or appear to work in jobs such as construction, landscaping, agriculture, or car washes that often do not require paperwork and are therefore attractive to illegal immigrants; and who do not speak much if any English. If the officers learn that the individual they stopped is a U. S. citizen or otherwise lawfully in the United States, they promptly let the individual go.

It's one thing to make up the law; it's entirely another thing to make up the facts. That's where we've arrived with the Trump Supreme Court. The justices' arguments are fiction, but their results are very real. Illegal secret police busts are now known as Kavanaugh stops because this clown of a justice thinks that the masked and armed officers behave like Mr. Rogers in combat gear. Never mind that the same Supreme Court ruled against using race to promote diversity in college admissions. Americans must be color blind when it comes to addressing racism but can rely on racism when it comes to terrorizing immigrants.

It took Justice Sonia Sotomayor to destroy the majority opinion and Kavanaugh's ludicrous legal gymnastics. She pointed out the facts: that armed and masked agents had seized individuals before asking any questions; that the Fourth Amendment had likely been violated because there can be no reasonable suspicion that is based on ethnicity, language, or the apparent place of work. "That decision is yet another grave misuse of our emergency docket," she wrote. "We should not have to live in a country where the Government can seize anyone who looks Latino, speaks Spanish, and appears to work a low wage job. Rather than stand idly by while our constitutional freedoms are lost, I dissent."

The people running Trump's secret police were naturally delighted with the ruling. "This is a win for the safety of Californians and the rule of law," said Department of Homeland Security Assistant Secretary Tricia McLaughlin. "DHS law enforcement will not be slowed down and will continue to arrest and remove the murderers, rapists, gang members, and other criminal illegal aliens." The DHS will also continue to arrest perfectly law-abiding immigrants who have legal status in this country, along with US citizens supposedly protected by the Bill of Rights. Those Californians, thrown in holding cells for hours on end, might be wondering what the rule of law actually means under the Trump Supreme Court.

* * *

The Supreme Court still has an aura of untouchability about it, as if it's glowing with some deep magisterial authority as consecrated by the Constitution. It's understandably hard to change the Constitution. So somehow, for some reason, we think, it must be hard to change the Supreme Court. Messing with the Supremes would surely disrupt the fragile balancing act that sustains the republic. They cannot be touched by mere mortals or else the whole system will come tumbling down. Except for the fact that conservatives have been messing with the Supreme Court since the Nixon era. They have gamed the system to install ideological hacks, conferring them with an institutional gravitas that masks their political agenda.

Just look at the results. Does anybody think that the ideological balance of the Court reflects that of the country? Trump's blowout majority in 2024, the highest water mark of Republicans nationwide in twenty years, was 1.5 percentage points. The national vote was almost evenly split, 49.8 percent to 48.3 percent. Yet on the highest court in the land, the split between conservatives and liberals is six to three: 67 percent to 33 percent.

That political chasm between the Court and the country explains why it has historically low ratings; just 50 percent of Americans say they have a favorable view of the Court, compared to 80 percent in the mid-1990s. As recently as 2021, even a majority of Democrats had a favorable view of the Supremes. That all changed when they decided to overturn *Roe v. Wade* and the federally mandated right to abortion.

The Supreme Court, of all institutions, should not care about polls. Still, at some point, its reputational legitimacy begins to crumble. The Court holds power only because it is seen as operating above politics, deciding constitutional matters along strictly legal lines. It has no actual means of enforcing its own decisions, just our collective respect for our nation's laws and system of government. According to the poll numbers, that respect is vanishing.

Even more alarming than the political chasm vis-à-vis the country is the judicial chasm between the Supreme Court and the federal court system beneath it. In the Trump era, with an administration that openly flouts the law, the conservative Supremes have taken extreme positions opposed to the vast majority of federal judges, including those appointed by Republican presidents by the name of Reagan, Bush, and, yes, Trump himself. Between May and June 2025, the federal courts ruled against the Trump administration 94.3 percent of the time, according to the Stanford University political scientist Adam Bonica. During that same period, the Supreme Court sided with the administration in 93.7 percent of the cases brought before it.

This Supreme Court has backstopped Trump in the dark, without public hearings or explanation, through a dramatic expansion of the shadow or emergency docket. Without explaining its rulings, the Court is failing to do its job; it leaves the lower courts with no guidance about the law. If a lower court tried to do the same, the Supreme Court would say that the federal judge had abused his or her power.

Not so long ago, the emergency docket was only rarely used for cases such as death row inmates facing execution—you know, *emergencies*. That has all changed, driven by Trump's lawlessness and the skewed politics of the Supremes. In the first twenty weeks of his second term, Trump made nineteen shadow docket applications. That's as many as Biden made in four years. The Obama and Bush administrations made only eight requests in their combined sixteen years.

Guess who won the vast majority of the shadow docket rulings? Trump has succeeded on the mass firings of government workers, the defunding of science based on sexual and racial bias, and those violent, racist immigration raids. The shadow docket is an express-lane power grab by the conservatives on the Court and the Trump White House. As Justice Elena Kagan wrote in September 2025, "Our emergency docket should never be used, as it has been this year, to permit what our own precedent bars. Still more, it should not be used, as it also has been, to transfer government authority from Congress to the President, and thus to reshape the Nation's separation of powers."

Federal judges have not held back in expressing their feelings about Trump's illegal conduct. Their sentiments are strikingly bipartisan across the several hundred lawsuits brought against his administration in just the first half of the first year of his return to office. Judge J. Harvie Wilkinson III, appointed by Reagan, said that Trump's refusal to return Kilmar Abrego Garcia from a brutal Salvadoran prison was "a path of perfect lawlessness, one that courts cannot condone." Judge Roger Gregory, appointed by George W. Bush, said that the notion that Venezuela had invaded the United States—the basis for the draconian immigration crackdown—was illegal. "As is becoming far too common, we are confronted again with the efforts of the Executive Branch to set aside the rule of law in pursuit of its goals," he wrote. Judge Richard Leon, also a Bush appointee, said this about Trump's executive order targeting the big law firm WilmerHale: "There is no doubt this retaliatory action chills speech and legal advocacy, or that it qualifies as a constitutional harm." Judge John Coughenour, appointed by Reagan, could barely contain his disdain for Trump's executive order denying citizenship to those born in this country. "I've been on the bench for over four decades," he said. "I can't remember another case where the question presented is as clear as this one. This is a blatantly unconstitutional order."

What is the Trumpian answer to all these searing judgments from the courts? Noncompliance and impeachment. Chad Mizelle, a Trump appointee in the Justice Department, told the November 2025 annual meeting of the right-wing Federalist Society that Congress needs to bring the federal courts into line. "What's going to force the Supreme Court to do something is fundamentally political pressure," he said. "It's going to be when Congress starts impeaching judges and saying, 'You are now encroaching into our territory.'" Mizelle was not just another official talking at just another conference. He was chief of staff to Attorney General Pam Bondi, and his wife serves as a Trump-appointed federal judge in Florida. Moreover, he was speaking to the most influential conservative legal group in the country, which has been extraordinarily successful in stacking the courts with its own right-wing ideologues.

To consider this Trump Supreme Court untouchable is to ignore the many ways its members have distorted the facts and the law to fit their own political goals. They barely hide their own political activism, even as they claim to stand against activist judges.

Back in January 2021, in the wake of the January 6 storming of the US Capitol, Justice Samuel Alito flew the flag of insurrection outside his home in Virginia. At the time, eleven days after the assault on our democracy, National Guard troops were still stationed outside Congress and even the Supreme Court itself. Even though there were numerous cases in front of his own court, Alito flew an upside-down American flag on his property. It was a blatant act of political support for Trump's attempts to overturn the free and fair election he had just lost.

Two years later, Alito was flying another January 6 flag outside his vacation home in New Jersey: the "Appeal to Heaven" flag featuring a pine tree. The flag is particularly beloved by the Christian nationalists who wanted to overturn the 2020 election in favor of Trump. Alito claimed that the upside-down flag was his wife's doing and that he had no involvement in what he portrayed as some kind of dispute with a provocative neighbor. He also claimed that the pine tree flag was flying because "my wife is fond of flying flags." Sure thing. Some wives enjoy baking; others express their solidarity with far-right theocrats seeking to overthrow the government by force. *Po-tay-to, po-tah-to.*

Yet Alito's public politicking didn't stop him from considering the case presented by Special Counsel Jack Smith. It didn't stop him from weighing in on the Court's landmark decision, just a few months before the 2024 election, about whether a president is immune from criminal prosecution.

Now, if Alito had been a federal district judge in a lower court, his flag-waving activism would have been a clear breach of the judicial code of conduct. Canon 5 of that code is titled "A Judge Should Refrain from Political Activity." That pretty much explains itself. In case there's any doubt, the Supreme Court's code of conduct uses similar language. There's just no way to enforce that code on the Supreme Court today. Beyond making speeches or running for office, "A Justice should not engage in other political activity." Above all, the Supremes' code of conduct states, as its first rule, that the justices "should maintain and observe high standards of conduct in order to preserve the integrity and independence of the federal judiciary." Samuel Alito preserves the independence of the judiciary about as well as Donald Trump preserved the East Wing of the White House.

He has company on the Court. Clarence Thomas, the longest-serving justice, is married to a conservative activist who was far more engaged in the effort to overturn the 2020 election results than Mrs. Alito was. In the weeks after Biden's victory, Ginni Thomas sent twenty-nine text messages to Trump's chief of staff, Mark Meadows, pushing false claims and conspiracy theories. She wanted the Trump White House to fight harder against Biden's win. She wanted it so badly that she attended the January 6 rally close to the White House that directly preceded the riot on Capitol Hill. She claimed that she left early and hadn't gone on to storm the Capitol because of the cold weather. Perhaps she had enough good sense to know that the optics of a sitting Supreme Court's wife storming the US Capitol wouldn't be great. Either that, or she was simply too cold.

Ginni Thomas has said that she doesn't discuss work with her husband. So it's just a coincidence that Thomas was the sole justice to dissent when the Supreme Court allowed a Democratic House committee to access Trump White House records about the January 6 insurrection in which Ginni's involvement was ultimately uncovered. It must have been an oversight that Justice Thomas refused to recuse himself from the case, when he surely knew that his wife was actively working with Republican officials to overturn the election results.

He must have known that his wife was on the board of CNP Action, a secretive right-wing group founded in 1981 to combat liberalism. At some point, even Clarence Thomas would have known that in the days after the 2020 election, CNP Action circulated a call to action, asking its members to contact legislators in three swing states that had voted for Joe Biden: Arizona, Georgia, and Pennsylvania. Its goal was simple: to keep Trump in power by appointing alternate slates of electors for the Electoral College, which formally votes for the president.

Ginni Thomas was busy on so many Trumpian fronts. She also founded the Groundswell activist group alongside Steve Bannon, Trump's onetime political guru. The group crafted what it called a "30-front war" on hot-button issues, delivering talking points to right-wing media, including Bannon's website, Breitbart News.

Back in 2011, Justice Thomas found his impartiality under attack because he attended a meeting of conservative donors sponsored by the Koch brothers, who were funding Tea Party groups. Ginni Thomas just happened to be heavily engaged with the Tea Party. The Supreme Court justice did not pretend that his wife had gone rogue, saying instead that they "believe in the same things." He claimed that his critics were "bent on undermining" the Supreme Court, as if he weren't undermining the Court himself. Thomas's expenses to attend the meeting were paid by the right-wing Federalist Society, which has been heavily supported by, yes, the Koch brothers.

Needless to say, the Thomases have a long relationship with the Heritage Foundation, which used to employ Mrs. Thomas as its liaison with the George W. Bush White House.

It's one thing to be partisan and unfair because of your activism; it's another thing entirely to make the Court look corrupt because of your moneygrubbing love of luxury. Between 2004 and 2023, Thomas accepted millions of dollars' worth of gifts, amounting to nearly twenty times the value of all the gifts received by all the other justices combined. He received more than two hundred gifts with a value of $4.2 million, according to a report by the reform group Fix the Court. That included several free luxury trips from Harlan Crow, a Dallas real estate developer who had cofounded the conservative Club for Growth, which pushes tax cuts wherever and whenever it can. Thomas also accepted free trips worth millions of dollars from other billionaires through the Horatio Alger Association. For context, all the other justices accepted a combined $248,000 from ninety-three gifts. And most of that was from the $170,000 accepted across sixteen gifts by Samuel Alito. It's funny how those strict originalist judges have so much trouble understanding the simple language of their own code of conduct.

In a statement, Thomas said that he had not disclosed the millions of dollars' worth of gifts because of "guidance from my colleagues and others in the judiciary." He claimed that those unnamed advisers had told him that "this sort of personal hospitality from close personal friends, who did not have business before the court, was not reportable."

That kind of excuse doesn't pass the smell test—and wouldn't stand up in a court of law. It doesn't even stand up to the public image that Thomas prefers to project: that of a simple man of the people. "I prefer the RV parks," he said in a documentary about his life funded by the same conservative donors who had gifted him all those luxury trips. "I prefer the Walmart parking lots to the beaches and things like that. There's something normal to me about it." Just a regular guy, that Clarence Thomas, a normal Walmart-loving regular passenger on private jets and yachts, traveling to private resorts all over the world. The kind of places you couldn't park your RV even if you had one.

What possible connection could exist between all those millions of dollars of gifts from conservative donors and the Supremes' decision to allow unlimited secret political donations in Citizens United in 2010? Corporations are people, too, especially if they have private jets that need filling. What possible connection could exist between all that political activism to overturn and oppose the 2020 election results and their decision in *Trump v. United States* in 2024? That's the case triggered by Trump's efforts to overturn the 2020 election results, including the January 6 insurrection. It's the one in which the conservative justices said that presidents have sweeping immunity from criminal prosecution for any "official acts"—such as inciting a riot to stop the democratic functions of an election.

This is our untouchable Supreme Court, the one that cannot be reformed because any political interference would surely taint a hallowed system of justice. And we couldn't possibly have that.

* * *

Reforming the Supreme Court is not only possible but necessary. It is justified by the justices' own behavior—especially if they threaten to undermine the very Constitution the justices are sworn to uphold and defend. That's not a matter of opinion; it's a matter of historical precedent, established by the man who shaped the nation as we know it: Abraham Lincoln, ranked time and again by historians as the greatest president in US history. Unless, of course, you ask Trump, who modestly ranks himself just slightly above our sixteenth president.

Lincoln appointed a tenth justice to the Court and made five appointments in all. Here's how and why.

His work to reform the Court started with the notorious Dred Scott decision in 1857, when a 7–2 majority ruled that Scott had no right to live as a free man. Scott had sued for his freedom, along with that of his wife and two daughters, because for four years they had lived in Illinois and Wisconsin, where slavery was illegal. Chief Justice Roger Taney wrote that African Americans could never be citizens and that the prohibition against slavery in the free states was unconstitutional because slave owners had been denied their property without due process.

Reaching for constitutional justification to deny the fundamental promise of the Constitution has a very long history. Due process for me, but not for thee.

The Dred Scott case was one more outrage that pushed the nation toward civil war. It also pushed the nation, after the war, to pass the Fourteenth Amendment, which guarantees citizenship to everyone born in this country—something Donald Trump wants to abolish.

Lincoln's first two Supreme Court nominations were to replace the two dissenters to the Dred Scott decision after one quit the Court and another passed away. He then replaced a third who had left the Court to join the Confederate war effort. That still left a majority of pro-slavery justices, so Lincoln added an extra seat—a tenth justice. The Constitution does not say how many justices should serve on the Court. The following year, the chief justice died, giving Lincoln the fifth appointment and thus half of the expanded Court.

That was not the end of the changes to the Supreme Court in the Civil War era. After Lincoln's assassination, his successor, Andrew Johnson, was a Unionist but also a white supremacist and former slave owner. Congress was rightly concerned that Johnson would roll back Reconstruction, so it limited his ability to appoint pro-slavery justices to the Court by reducing its number to seven. Once Johnson left office, Congress restored the Court to nine justices, where it stands today.

How could Lincoln justify tampering with the Court like that? When he became president, seven southern states had already seceded from the Union. Yet half the Court's justices, including the chief justice, were southerners. The Court did not reflect the political consensus of the nation. It even threatened to undermine Lincoln's war effort. The same racist chief justice challenged the wartime suspension of habeas corpus, the core protection for citizens against arbitrary arrest or detention. Lincoln held his ground, because he wanted to be able to detain Americans suspected of aiding the Confederacy. The Court was powerless to stop him.

In other words, Lincoln reformed the Supreme Court to hold the country together. He changed its makeup to establish the core freedoms for all Americans that sit at the heart of the Declaration of Independence and the Constitution.

If you think we don't face existential challenges as a democratic republic today, you'll think it's crazy to tamper with the Supreme Court. But ask yourself if we're still a democracy when masked secret police can arrest and detain our fellow citizens because of the color of their skin or their place of work. Ask yourself if we're still a democracy when the highest court in the land thinks it's acceptable to ignore the facts, the decisions of hundreds of fellow judges, and the Constitution itself. Ask yourself if we're still a democracy when the highest court issues its decisions without a single hearing and without explanation. Ask yourself if we're still a democracy when the highest court can include political activists, bought by rich donors, who keep secret their millions of dollars of gifts to the justices.

To restore democracy, to restore integrity to the judicial system, we urgently need to reform the Supreme Court. Those reforms need to be based on principle, not politics, to have any legitimacy or public support. The first order of a filibuster-free Congress should be reform of the Supreme Court. Not the second or the third or the fourth, or it will be too late to save the republic and our independent judiciary. If any subsequent reforms are to stand a chance at surviving, we cannot leave in place a rogue branch of government with the power to strike down anything that doesn't comport with its far-right ideology.

The first reform should be to expand the Court, in line with the principles that determined the number of justices in the early years of the republic. The first Supreme Court had six justices, reflecting the six federal court circuits. The Court grew to seven justices in 1807, after a seventh circuit was added. It grew again to nine after two new circuits were added in 1837. Today there are thirteen federal court circuits but only nine Supreme Court justices. The Court should reflect the size of the country and the scope of its legal challenges, as it did more than a century ago.

The second reform should be to limit the term of new justices to eight years, allowing newly elected presidents to choose their own nominees regularly. This would reduce the opportunities for the kind of procedural delays that stymied Obama's appointment of a justice in his final year in office. The regular flow of new appointments would help remove the national drama from each nomination by diluting the novelty of each new appointment. Once again, there is widespread public support for term limits for Supreme Court justices: 75 percent of Americans agree with term limits, according to a PRRI survey in 2025.

The third reform should be to establish an enforceable code of conduct, with a Supreme Court panel mandated to investigate allegations of wrongdoing and impropriety. The panel should have the power to force the recusal of justices in cases where they have personal ties and even force the removal of justices in cases of conduct unworthy of the Supreme Court. Public polling suggests that there is huge support for such reforms as well: 76 percent of Americans are in favor of a binding code of conduct, according to a *USA Today* poll in 2024.

The final reform should be to retire any justice over the age of seventy from the Supreme Court, regardless of who appointed them. The Constitution says that judges "shall hold their Offices during good Behaviour," which has been interpreted as lifetime appointments. That is one way to interpret the phrase but by no means the only one. A retired Supreme Court justice could be moved to a lower court and still stay within a reasonable interpretation of the constitutional language.

In fact, there's widespread public support for retiring all public officials over a certain age, and there's a surprising degree of consensus on what that age should be. As many as 79 percent of Americans favor age limits for elected officials, and 74 percent favor them for Supreme Court justices, according to Pew Research Center. Polling by the Benenson Strategy Group in 2022 showed that a clear majority—63 percent of Democrats and 55 percent of Republicans—support an upper age limit of seventy for anyone to be sworn in as president. (The Constitution does not set any age range for the Supreme Court but does state that the presidency has a lower age limit of thirty-five.)

Mandatory retirement at seventy years of age would lead to four immediate vacancies on the Supreme Court: three conservatives and one liberal. Clarence Thomas and Samuel Alito would leave, along with Chief Justice John Roberts. So would Sonia Sotomayor, appointed by Barack Obama. All three Trump judges would remain, along with one Obama and one Biden appointee.

Ever since Franklin D. Roosevelt tried and failed to expand the

Supreme Court, Washington has shied away from reforming the highest court in the land. However, FDR's plan was the product of another political era, almost a century ago. The Court had struck down several pieces of his New Deal plan to revive the economy from the depths of the Great Depression. FDR also proposed to retire judges at age seventy, but if they refused to leave, he would be free to add an additional justice, potentially expanding the Court to fifteen. Congress defeated his plan, but FDR ultimately prevailed; within five years, seven of the nine justices were his own appointees.

Today's Supreme Court has weakened itself by its political activism, repeatedly disregarding the Constitution and its code of conduct. It is populated by older justices at a time when the American people are yearning to reform the status quo. If we want to revive our democracy, we need to revive our Supreme Court. If that seems extreme, consider an alternative that is already upon us: a Court that undermines the very Constitution it's supposed to uphold.

5

We the People

North Carolina is a competitive purple state that leans Republican. Trump won it in 2024 by a margin of 2.2 percent, and both of its US senators won their seats by similar margins in the previous two election cycles. In 2022, its congressional districts were aligned with a map drawn up by a court-appointed special master. The result was what you might expect from a battleground state: seven Republicans and seven Democrats.

However, in that same election, Republicans won a majority on the state's highest court and set about ripping up the nonpartisan map. Two years later, North Carolina elected ten Republicans and just four Democrats. That was in a cycle in which the overall House of Representatives barely changed its makeup across the country.

If you're a Democratic voter in North Carolina, your vote in 2024 was worth much, much less than it was in 2022. Democrats in North Carolina won 46 percent of the votes in congressional races in 2024 but just 29 percent of the congressional seats. The manipulated maps created districts that were completely lopsided apart from one. Every Republican won by double digits. With the exception of a single seat, Democrats won their three districts by between 35 and 48 percent.

This means that there is almost no room for a competitive contest in one of the most competitive states in the country.

If you think that was a shameless distortion of democracy, you should see the maps for 2026. That single, narrowly won Democratic district? It's gone as part of Trump's campaign to engineer guaranteed victory for House Republicans in the midterms. What's worse, they're not even trying to hide it. State Senator Phil Berger, a Republican, posted the new map on X, saying that the North Carolina General Assembly was "ready to help Republicans secure Congress and move @realDonaldTrump's agenda forward!"

Across the country in 2024, by gerrymandering electoral maps, Republicans manipulated an extra sixteen House seats into their column when compared to fair electoral maps, according to analysis by the Brennan Center for Justice. Those seats just happened to be in parts of the country where Joe Biden won the presidential vote in 2020.

How have Republicans managed to skew democracy so much? Because they pursue power over principle, whereas too many Democrats pursue fairness and good government. Republicans controlled the drawing of 191 of the districts in 2024, compared to only 75 controlled by Democrats. The rest of the House districts were drawn by commissions, courts, or divided state governments. In the Democratic strongholds of California and New York, there are independent redistricting commissions. In Texas and Florida, there is no such thing. In Republican-controlled districts, there is little legal recourse to correct the maps. In their largely conservative courts, the judges often refrain from interfering with map schemes—unlike the mostly liberal courts reviewing maps in Democratic districts.

That was happening well before Trump realized that his best hope for keeping control of the House was not to win the midterm elections in 2026 but to win the maps. "I got the highest vote in the history of Texas," he told CNBC as he pushed Texas to start the gerrymandering war. "We are entitled to five more seats."

It's true that Trump easily won the Electoral College votes in

Texas, by a margin of 13.5 percent. But it's also true that 43 percent of the state's voters voted for Kamala Harris. Before Trump pushed his scheme to distort democracy, Democrats had won 41 percent of the House districts in Texas.

So what exactly was he entitled to? According to Steve Bannon, Trump's soulmate in seizing power, the stakes are personal, as usual. "This redistricting war is the opening salvo of a battle that must be won," he told *The New York Times* in November 2025. "We must have these victories. If Trump doesn't hold the House, they will impeach him. It will be a nightmare and a blood bath."

What do you call a political system that changes its election rules just to protect its leader from investigation and accountability? It's certainly not a democracy as we've known it. Can a country still call itself a democracy if its leader is ready to sacrifice democratic elections to protect himself?

The rapid descent into autocracy began, of course, with the Trump Supreme Court, in a North Carolina case decided in October 2018, during Trump's first term. The case, *Rucho v. Common Cause*, involved another Republican-dominated map. "I think electing Republicans is better than electing Democrats," said David Lewis, one of the map's architects. "So I drew this map to help foster what I think is better for the country." Subtle.

Confronted with such blatant election rigging, the Supreme Court decided that it was powerless to intervene. Judges, according to the highest judge in the land, did not have the authority or the skill to decide when politics was messing too much with democracy. "We conclude that partisan gerrymandering claims present political questions beyond the reach of the federal courts," John Roberts wrote. How foolish of us to think that judges might be capable of passing judgment.

That nonsense was called out by the liberal minority. "For the first time ever, this Court refuses to remedy a constitutional violation because it thinks the task beyond judicial capabilities," wrote Justice Kagan. ". . . These gerrymanders enabled politicians to entrench themselves in office as against voters' preferences. They promoted partisanship above respect for the popular will. They encouraged a politics of polarization and dysfunction. If left unchecked, gerrymanders like the ones here may irreparably damage our system of government."

Such map redrawing schemes were deepened and extended across the country five years later, as Trump leaned on every Republican governor he could find.

Redrawing congressional maps normally happens after the national census, at the start of every decade. To redraw the maps in mid-decade, just a year before a national election, is unprecedented. Because the highest court in the land says it's powerless and clueless, the door is now open for every president to lean on every like-minded governor to try to manipulate every national election.

It took a game of cat and mouse by Texas Democrats to get the nation to pay attention to our slide into autocracy. When Trump pushed Texas Governor Greg Abbott, a Republican, to redraw the state's districts—to give Republicans five more House seats—it seemed like just another MAGA break from the norm. It wasn't. Abbott called a special session of the legislature to ram through his plan to prop up Trump, claiming that he was just giving Texans the chance to vote for the candidate of their choice. He even claimed that he was forced to gerrymander because of a technical ruling by an appeals court on the Voting Rights Act—as if the logical conclusion of civil rights legislation was to devalue the votes of Black and Latino communities.

That was when Texas Democrats blocked the governor's political scheme—for a while—using their only recourse left: leaving the state and thus denying the legislature a quorum. "We all feel so strongly that this power grab is so brazen, so egregious, so dangerous for the future of our republic that we had no other choice but to make this stand," State Representative James Talarico told me. "I hope it inspires not just all Texans but all Americans to step up and do something to stop this power grab from happening."

It was only a temporary protest, but it exposed the true nature of the Republicans' power lust. The speaker of the Texas House of Representatives issued civil arrest warrants and imposed daily fines. The governor asked the state's top court to remove the Democrats from office, even though the process would have taken forever and only led to new elections in safe Democratic seats. Texas Senator John Cornyn, a Republican, asked the FBI to locate the lawmakers, even though there were no federal crimes involved.

So much for the legislators' commitment to democracy. The excessive threats underscored the fact that the gerrymander was nothing more than a power grab. Still, the heavy-handed tactics served to reawaken a progressive movement that had been cowed by Trump's return to power. Thousands of people protested in cities across the country, with the biggest demonstration at the Texas Capitol in Austin. "Do not allow this moment to pass without a fight," said Beto O'Rourke of El Paso, a Democratic former congressman.

It didn't. The Trump scheme and the progressive protests triggered the most important pushback of all: California's redistricting, led by Governor Gavin Newsom. "You've got to fight fire with fire," Newsom told me. "This is an existential moment. We have agency. We can act superior. We can act holier than thou and watch the last half century wiped out in real time. I think we need to be held to a higher level of accountability, meet this moment, lean in on this, and get tough."

The California map carves out five more Democratic-leaning districts to counter the five new Republican-leaning districts in Texas. But the path to doing so in California required something unnecessary in Texas: the consent of the people. Because of previous efforts to eliminate gerrymandering, using maps drawn by an independent commission, Newsom's response needed voters to support a ballot measure. Allowing Americans to have a say: imagine that.

The campaign wasn't easy or cheap. The "Yes on 50" campaign raised more than $100 million to convince California voters to support what Newsom called the Election Rigging Response Act and Proposition 50, named for all the states in the union. (Full disclosure:

My "Yes on 50" livestream raised a million dollars for the campaign.) Against the change were Republicans including former Governor Arnold Schwarzenegger, and the wealthy heir Charles Munger, who spent more than $30 million to stop Newsom. The result was a massive win for what Newsom called "fighting fire with fire"—an almost two-to-one margin of victory for the new California maps. "We need our friends in New York, in Illinois, in Colorado—we need to see other states, with their remarkable leaders, that have been doing remarkable things, to meet this moment head-on as well," Newsom said on election night 2025.

A few days after winning voter support for the new maps, Newsom was in Houston, Texas, for a rally with state Democratic leaders. "You woke us up," he told the Texas Democrats. "You didn't just have your back here. You had our back in the state of California."

* * *

Why is Donald Trump obsessed with the 2020 election? Because he lost. He's a loser. He was beaten like a drum, as Joe Biden predicted. It wasn't even close. Biden beat him by a margin of 4.5 percent of the national vote—a far bigger win than the 1.5 percent margin Trump scraped out over Kamala Harris four years later. Biden won 81 million votes, 4 million more than Trump in 2024, and 18 million more than Trump in 2016. The man Trump derided as a doddering old fool was far more popular than the supposedly populist former TV star.

In the twilight zone bizarro world that is Trump's head, that means something was wrong with our elections. Trump may genuinely believe his own Big Lie at this point. Or it may be just a ploy to rig future elections in his party's favor. It's hard to understand the inane thought processes of an incoherent autocrat.

Whatever the explanation, Trump decided to declare war on mail-in ballots because they were one way to explain why he had been such a loser in 2020. Granted, this makes absolutely no sense if you look at the facts of mail-in voting. When Trump started to trash mail-in voting in

2020, some political scientists at the University of Virginia decided to look at the data. They studied voting behavior in counties with universal mail-in voting and compared them to those without. Some states, including Oregon, Washington, Utah, Colorado, and Hawaii, have switched almost exclusively to voting by mail. That means there were 175 counties with universal mail-in voting compared to 3,000 without in the 2018 data the researchers studied. The result: All-mail voting increased turnout by between 1.8 and 2.9 percent among all voters. The advantage to Democrats was so tiny in their study—0.7 percent—that it fell within the margin of statistical error. Another study, by Stanford University researchers, looked at counties that had switched to all-mail ballots in 2006, 2012, and 2018. They found an even smaller Democratic advantage of 0.1 percent.

What happened in 2020 was exceptional—and occurred because of Trump's stupidity. Because he trashed mail-in ballots, there was a highly unusual gap between Democrats and Republicans where there had normally been none: 58 percent of Democrats voted by mail compared to 29 percent of Republicans. That should come as no surprise to Donald Trump or the nation, given how he talked about mail-in voting during the final stages of the election. "There is fraud," he said during his TV debate with Biden in September 2020. "They found them in creeks. They found them with the name Trump in a wastepaper basket. This will be a fraud like you have never seen." The only fraud was Trump himself. As Biden pointed out, Trump voted by mail-in ballot from the Oval Office, sending his ballot to Florida.

What happened four years later was obviously a miracle, because during the 2024 election under the Biden presidency, mail-in votes for Trump were astonishingly not dumped into creeks and trash cans—unlike the mail-in votes during his own presidency.

In 2024, Republicans erased the Democrats' advantage in mail-in voting in nearly every state that tracks party registration, according to an analysis by *The New York Times*. In fact, in the battleground state of Arizona, Republicans even gained an 8-point lead over Democrats in mail-in voting. In Pennsylvania, Republicans halved the gap with Democrats in mail-in voting.

Despite the facts and the votes, the Trump Supreme Court decided to examine the counting of mail-in ballots received after election day. The case pitted the state of Mississippi, not exactly a bastion of Democratic power, against the Republican National Committee. Mississippi gives a five-day grace period, similar to that of many other states, to allow election officials to count ballots that arrive in the mail a few days after election day.

Bear in mind that if the RNC had beef with Mississippi's election laws, it could've simply lobbied the state legislature to change its laws prior to the election. After all, Republicans held a majority in the Mississippi House of Representatives and a supermajority in the Mississippi Senate. However, the lawsuit served a dual purpose. If successful, it would strike down the grace period. But it was also a vehicle to ultimately render illegal any ballots that arrive after election day across the country. And what better bet for Republicans than a lawsuit heard by a judge in ruby red Mississippi, contained within the überconservative Fifth Circuit?

Never mind that Mississippi had voted for Trump by a margin of 22 points the last time around. Never mind that the Constitution says very clearly that "The Times, Places and Manner of holding Elections" are for the states to decide. If Trump says that something is wrong, it must be wrong, regardless of the facts or the law. This is Trump's insurance policy for elections. If he wins an election, it's fair and free. If he loses, it's fraud. Heads he wins, tails you lose.

For that to work, Trump needs some flexibility in how elections are managed—just enough leeway to fix the results the way he wants them. That's why he issued a totally illegal executive order just a couple of months into his second term in a brazen attempt to take control of elections across the country. He claimed the entirely fabricated and unconstitutional power to regulate federal elections, ignoring all the state governments as well as Congress. The order requires voters to produce a passport or similar document to register to vote. Only around half of Americans even hold a passport. Those who don't are disproportionately minorities, low-income people, or simply younger Americans—all of which are demographics that *just happen* to skew Democratic. The order goes on to say that the United States Election Assistance Commission, an independent and bipartisan agency, needs to decertify its voting machines, currently used in thirty-nine states. Confusion over which machines are valid would give Trump a lot of flexibility to question any election results he doesn't much like. The order also pretends to force the states to stop counting mail-in ballots received after election day.

The order was followed by the SAVE Act, which purports to protect elections by requiring voters to prove their citizenship. That means voters would need a passport (costing $165), which many Americans don't already possess and can't afford. It is, in effect, a poll tax by another name. Voters could alternatively show a birth certificate, but that would not suffice for anyone who changed their name since birth. In case anyone is confused about the main reason for the proposed new law, it also forces states to share voter rolls with the Department of Homeland Security. Voter suppression is the opposite of protecting elections. But it's such a big priority for Trump that he insisted on blocking all other legislation unless and until the SAVE Act was passed. He even wanted to nuke the Senate filibuster to get it done.

This is just the latest in a long line of Republicans' vote-rigging efforts. For years, they have been closing polling sites across the South in districts dominated by voters of color. If it's harder to vote, voters tend not to show up in the same numbers. The scheme really gained traction after conservatives on the Supreme Court ruled in 2013 that the states covered by the Voting Rights Act—the ones that clung to Jim Crow—no longer needed federal clearance to change their voting laws. According to the conservative Supremes, that was an unconstitutional case of the federal government trampling on state rights.

In the first five years after the 2013 ruling in *Shelby County v.*

Holder, 1,688 polling places were closed down across thirteen states, many of them in southern Black communities. Texas alone closed 750 polling sites, according to research by the Leadership Conference on Civil and Human Rights. In Dallas County, which is 41 percent Latino and 22 percent African American, there were 74 closures. In Arizona, 320 sites were closed, including 171 in Maricopa County, which is 31 percent Latino. If you're wondering why you always see long lines of voters in communities of color, now you know why.

Trump's home state of Florida has been at the forefront of some of the worst election rigging. Instead of squeezing the voting process, the state's MAGA mob has squeezed the voter rolls. For years, Florida has gamed its elections by denying voting rights to anyone with a felony conviction. Between 2010 and 2016—the Obama years, naturally— the number of voters purged this way grew to 1.68 million. That included more than one in five of the state's Black voting-age population. For context, Trump won the state of Florida in 2016 by just 113,000 votes.

Two years later, Florida voters overwhelmingly approved a constitutional amendment to restore voting rights to most people with felony convictions after they complete their sentence—with the exception of murder or sex offenses. But who cares about democracy when you're a Republican governor trying to out-MAGA Trump in a presidential primary? Within months, Ron DeSantis signed a bill requiring those newly restored voters to pay off their court debts before being allowed to vote. The only problem? There is no central system telling people what they might owe, so the result was widespread confusion. But Republicans didn't stop there. The state legislature also passed laws to pursue alleged voting fraud aggressively, including the creation of a partisan election police unit. Naturally the police arrested people with past felony convictions who genuinely thought they were eligible to vote. Some had even received voter information cards from the state. Heads they win again, tails you lose again.

Here's the five-step plan to steal elections. The first step is to pretend that the other side stole an election, in 2020 for instance. The second is to tilt the playing field by rigging electoral maps, purging voter rolls, and closing polling sites. The third is to sow enough confusion into the voting process to cast doubt on any part of the election: voter registration, mail-in ballots, voting machines. The fourth is to stack the highest court in the land with your ideological cronies to rubber-stamp your steal. The fifth is to shout louder than anyone else, to drown out the very concept of truth. That's how you end a democracy in five Trumpy steps. If only it were merely theoretical.

* * *

The only way to rebuild our democracy is for a new Congress to pass sweeping laws to do just that. Democrats came close to doing so in 2021, passing the Freedom to Vote Act through the House and winning a majority in the Senate—but not enough to beat back the Republican filibuster. When the filibuster is used to block democracy and basic constitutional rights, you know it should play no role in shaping the country.

Let's be honest. There's no *legitimate reason* why Republicans should make it hard for Americans to vote. There's virtually zero fraud. More voters mean both more Republicans and more Democrats at the polls. The only reason to block the legislation is that voter suppression and election denial have been successful strategies for seizing power. As it happens, a supermajority of Americans support the pro-democracy legislation: 70 percent of likely voters backed it, including the vast majority of Republicans.

The Freedom to Vote Act expands access to voting by requiring all fifty states to offer early voting periods for at least two weeks prior to election day. Early voting sites would need to be within walking distance of public transport, as well as on college campuses. It ensures that mail-in ballots are available for all voters and can arrive within seven days of election day. It allows for a wide range of voter identification in states that require it, not just an expensive passport. And it makes election day a federal holiday, making it much more practical for working people to vote.

Voter registration would be made much easier. The national standard would be automatic voter registration, such as when people obtain a driver's license. Same-day voter registration, already available in twenty-two states and Washington, DC, would be extended across the country. Perhaps most important, purges of voting rolls would be less open to abuse, and purged voters would need to be notified within forty-eight hours, giving them information about how to challenge their removal. Voting rights would be restored to citizens who were formerly incarcerated.

To counter the widespread closure of polling sites in minority communities, states would need to ensure that voting lines last no longer than thirty minutes. They would also be forbidden from stopping donations of food and water to voters standing in line, as some states have done.

There would be a ban on partisan gerrymandering with clear rules for redistricting and judicial remedies for manipulated maps. That would presumably be a welcome solution for all those Republicans clutching their pearls amid California's map redraw. There would be added protections for local election officials to prevent their firings for partisan reasons, as well as penalties for destroying ballots or election records.

Finally, the legislation would require disclosure of anyone donating more than $10,000 in a cycle, ending the days of dark money secretly flooding our elections. Political action committees known as super PACs would need to work independently, not just fake the appearance of independence from a campaign or candidate. These may be small measures to deal with the tidal wave of money in our elections, but they are a start at reform.

Thoughts and prayers are not enough to defend what's left of our democracy or rebuild what Trump and the MAGA mob have destroyed. Until democracy stands up for itself, until we fight for our system of government, we cannot hope to protect free and fair elections in our own country.

That includes being honest with ourselves about the relic of the founders' idealism known as the Electoral College. It remains distorted by the original sin of compromise with southern slaveholders, leaving small states with disproportionate numbers of electors. A majority of Americans have wanted to abolish it since the 1960s, and there have been more proposals for constitutional amendments about it than any other subject. Yet they have all failed. It remains the weakest link in our weakened democracy, vulnerable to abuse by the very type of demagogue the founders wanted to exclude from the presidency, the kind of wannabe tyrant who would concoct a scheme of fake electors by interfering with the certification process with something like an insurrection at the Capitol. In the absence of a constitutional amendment, the best reform to protect our democracy would be the National Popular Vote Interstate Compact, an agreement among states to vote for the winner of the national popular vote. To be effective, it would need states representing 270 Electoral College votes to adopt the compact. As of now, states with 209 votes have signed up. Legislative chambers in states with another 74 votes have voted for the compact but not finished the job. Reform of the Electoral College is not a far-fetched idea for the distant future; it could become reality sooner than you think.

For decades American officials have traveled the globe to monitor elections and advise other governments on how to promote democracy. It's no coincidence that Trump canceled those programs and his officials ordered our diplomats to shut their mouths about the dictators and autocrats we have traditionally opposed. Marco Rubio likes to criticize dictatorships in Venezuela, Belarus, and Russia. But as a matter of policy, as Trump's secretary of state and possible MAGA successor, he thinks that's a bad idea. In an official cable to US diplomats in the summer of 2025, he said that they "should avoid opining on the fairness or integrity of an electoral process, its legitimacy, or the democratic values of the country in question." He helpfully explained that the diplomats should not use their election statements "to promote an ideology."

That ideology would be the very American one of democracy.

"Put another way," he wrote, "would the president say it?" Of course Trump wouldn't criticize another autocrat for rigging an election—because that's been his own project in the homeland for many, many years. Neither Trump nor Rubio can afford to be embarrassed by US diplomats standing up for American values. So they need to tell them to zip it if they want to keep their jobs.

That's why it's vital to make the Freedom to Vote legislation a national priority for the next president—not something to defer and delay, as two Democratic senators did. The defense of democracy is a battle we cannot afford to ignore or avoid.

It was Ronald Reagan, the first president to campaign on the slogan about making America great again, who defined the stakes for us today. "Freedom . . . is never more than one generation away from extinction," he said in his first inaugural address as California governor in January 1967. ". . . It must be fought for and defended constantly by each generation."

This is our generation's fight for freedom: the fight for our own democratic elections.

6

Not a King

I'm not a king. I'm not a king," said the man who claims unchecked power to run the country, extort millions of dollars from corporations, and ignore the Constitution. "I work my ass off to make our country great. That's all it is. I'm not a king at all."

Trump was talking to reporters on board Air Force One as the No Kings protests fanned out across the United States in June 2025. It's true that he has not enjoyed a coronation at the National Cathedral and does not claim a hereditary line of succession (yet). But it's also true that he has often claimed the very powers of a king that the framers of the Constitution were so determined to oppose.

Just two months before he swore that he was not a king, Trump told his cabinet members that he had unlimited power to send troops into any city in any state—especially into Chicago, where Illinois Governor JB Pritzker had called him a wannabe dictator. "Not that I don't have—I would—the right to do anything I want to do," Trump said. "I'm the president of the United States. If I think our country is in danger—and it is in danger in these cities—I can do it."

In that same meeting, he mused that maybe the American people actually wanted a dictator, not a president. Not that he was a dictator, you understand. Even though he had said he wanted to be a dictator on day one of his presidency. "So the line is that I'm a dictator, but I stop crime," he explained. "So a lot of people say, 'If that's the case, I'd rather have a dictator.' But I'm not a dictator. I just know how to stop crime.

". . . You have a guy in Illinois, the governor of Illinois, saying that crime has been much better in Chicago recently, and Trump is a dictator. And most people say, 'If you call him a dictator, then if he stops crime, he can be whatever he wants.' I'm not a dictator, by the way. But he can be whatever he wants."

It was just the latest in a long line of kinglike eruptions from the great leader. Back in his first term, he told Charlie Kirk's right-wing student group, Turning Point USA, that the Constitution actually gave him "the right to do whatever I want as president."

It is the literal definition of a dictator to be a ruler with absolute and unrestricted power over a country. A dictator issues diktats, or decrees, that must be obeyed without question or challenge, no matter how unfair. Like the ones bullying the nation's private universities into stopping their programs promoting diversity and environmental justice. Or the ones bullying the nation's largest law firms by terminating their federal contracts and suspending their security clearances to stop working with clients such as George Soros and start working for free for Donald Trump.

You'd think the MAGA Republicans would mind licking the boots of a dictator, based on their past attacks on a previous president who issued executive orders. But that president was Barack Obama a decade earlier, so obviously it was completely different. "I think it's divisive and quite frankly borderline unconstitutional," Marco Rubio said about Obama's promise to use executive orders in his State of the Union address in 2014. "I understand the process takes a long time and can be frustrating, but I think it truly undermines the republic." Lindsey Graham, one of Trump's most devoted fans, said that Obama was making a big mistake. "I think he's going to create an impression among the American people that he's abusing the power of his office and that will hurt Democrats," said the South Carolina senator. His fellow South Carolina senator, Tim Scott, was a bit more blunt: "We continue to erode the whole notion of the rule of law." John Boehner, the Republican speaker of the House at the time, said that Obama was acting "like a king or emperor." Ted Cruz of Texas said that Obama had created an imperial presidency. "Rule of law doesn't simply mean that society has laws; dictatorships are often characterized by an abundance of laws," he wrote in *The Wall Street Journal*. "Rather, rule of law means that we are a nation ruled by laws, not men. That no one—and especially not the president—is above the law."

How painfully, obviously, embarrassingly true.

It's worth noting that Obama signed 277 executive orders in eight years. Trump signed nearly that many (226) in just the first year of his second term. Combined with another 220 during his first term, he's on track to more than double the number "Emperor Obama" signed. Yet there has been nary a word of dissent from Rubio, Graham, Cruz, or any other Republican.

The notion of an imperial presidency was coined by the historian Arthur M. Schlesinger, Jr., in response to Richard Nixon's abuses of power. Those abuses included waging war without congressional approval and declaring national emergencies to dodge constitutional limits on power. It's no coincidence that Trump has declared national emergencies to justify everything from his immigration raids to his military strikes in the Caribbean. Other emergencies have justified everything from his global tariffs to mining on federal lands.

Nixon had the temerity and arrogance to redesign the White House security uniforms to look like those of European honor guards, complete with gold braid and marching band hats. They looked like a palace guard and were widely ridiculed in the media as worthy of a banana republic. *The New York Times* called them "operetta-like." The uniforms lasted just a few months before the laughing irritated Nixon too much and the security personnel went back to their old uniforms.

You can't say the same for the historic East Wing of the White House, which Trump decided to demolish, on a whim, without consultation, to make room for a $400 million gilded ballroom. (At least, it was $400 million at the time of this writing, after escalating from $200 million to $300 million and then $350 million along the way.) Yes, it's just a building. No, it's not the most shocking abuse of power under the Trump regime. But it does embody the many shades of the imperial presidency of Donald Trump in one simple image of a backhoe ripping down the stately facade of American power.

First there was the brazen lying: just two months before the wholesale demolition, Trump said that his precious ballroom "won't interfere with the current building." That was followed by the brazen cover-up as he pretended—after the building was ripped down—that "the East Wing is being fully modernized as part of this process." In between there was the secret fundraising from corporate executives with business in front of the Trump administration, including the defense giant Lockheed Martin, the surveillance giant Palantir, and the tech titans Google, Meta, Apple, Amazon, and Microsoft.

The White House would have you believe that lots of other presidents have done similar things. Not even close. When Harry Truman renovated the place in the 1940s, it was structurally unsound. At one point, his daughter's piano fell through the floor. Truman worked with Congress, appointed a bipartisan commission to oversee the project, and consulted with the American Society of Civil Engineers and the Commission of Fine Arts. They approved the White House architect's plans, and the funds were approved by Congress itself. Trump has consulted nobody; shown detailed plans to nobody in public; bypassed Congress entirely.

The demolition does not just involve the East Wing, where the First Lady traditionally works with her senior staff. Buried under the East Wing is the Presidential Emergency Operations Center, an underground bunker built to withstand an aerial attack, complete with modern communications to run the government in time of war. It's where Vice President Dick Cheney and Bush's senior team were stationed during the terrorist attacks of September 11, 2001. It's where Trump himself hid during the George Floyd protests of May 2020. The bunker is so sensitive that when the Bush administration wanted to update the bunker after 9/11, the construction was done entirely in secret. Officials would say only that the construction was "underground work" to fix electrical and plumbing problems. By the time the big dig was under way, in 2010, the cost was $376 million and the renovations stretched from the East Wing to the West Wing. It took two years and was surrounded by privacy screens. Even the contractor companies were required to cover up their logos in what was simply called "security-related construction."

Now the White House is run by a man who declares that the nation is under attack from immigrants but doesn't care about exposing his own presidential bunker. But hey, what's the value of national security compared to a thousand-person ballroom?

We've been told again and again that Trump is a populist leader. He connects with working Americans. He won his second term by attacking his predecessor for the high price of groceries. For the price of a single egg. Then he spent his first year back in power slapping gold paint all over the Oval Office, including a gold-painted sign outside its door. He paved over the Rose Garden to make it look like his Mar-a-Lago patio. He has his eye on building a triumphal arch—the Arc de Trump—opposite the Lincoln Memorial. Because nothing says "man of the people" quite like surrounding yourself with enough gold to make Liberace blush.

It took former First Lady Michelle Obama to explain the meaning of Trump's destruction. "When we talk about the East Wing, it is the heart of the work," she told *Vanity Fair* about her old offices. "And to denigrate it, to tear it down, to pretend like it doesn't matter—it's a reflection of how you think of that role."

In response, Trump pretended that he had somehow been forced to demolish the place. "It looked like hell," he said. "I didn't want to sacrifice a great ballroom for an okay ballroom by leaving it right smack in the middle."

Who could put up with an okay ballroom when a great ballroom is so, so close? Certainly not a king. Not a king at all.

* * *

There is one kinglike power the framers wrote into the Constitution. Naturally, Donald Trump has done his very best to abuse it. The president has the "power to grant Reprieves and Pardons for Offences against the United States, except in Cases of Impeachment." Pardon power is an old prerogative of English kings, dating back to the seventh century. It's supposed to be an act of mercy, covering a range of options from commutation of a sentence to amnesty for a whole group of people. George Washington issued an amnesty for those involved in Pennsylvania's Whiskey Rebellion. Abraham Lincoln used it to encourage desertions from the Confederate Army. His successor, Andrew Johnson, pardoned Jefferson Davis, the defeated president of the Confederacy, which was surely the most controversial pardon until Gerald Ford pardoned Richard Nixon in 1974.

That's not to say that recent presidents have not made questionable pardons. George H. W. Bush pardoned those involved in the Iran-Contra scandal, saying that policy differences had become criminal matters. On his last day in office, Bill Clinton pardoned the fugitive financier Marc Rich, whose ex-wife just happened to be a major Democratic donor. Then there was Joe Biden's pardon of his son, Hunter, after repeatedly saying he wouldn't pardon him.

None of those recent presidents comes close to the pardon abuses of Donald Trump. They are not in the same universe of corruption, disregard for the rule of law, political manipulation, and sheer incompetence.

Just a few months into office, Trump pardoned a MAGA fan in Nevada named Michele Fiore. She had been convicted of stealing money collected for a statue honoring a murdered police officer. If you think that's a disgusting thing to do, just wait until you hear what she spent the money on: cosmetic surgery, rent, and her daughter's wedding. To be clear, the $70,000 statue campaign was for two officers who were having a pizza lunch when an antigovernment husband and wife shot them, leaving a note promising the start of a revolution.

Remember: Trump likes to sell himself as the anticrime crusader, a champion for the nation's police officers. But he pardoned someone who had ripped off a memorial to two fallen officers—and spent the money on herself. In addition to being a MAGA wing nut, Fiore is an actual justice of the peace for the city of Pahrump and a committee-woman for the Nevada Republican Party.

Trump has a particular soft spot for corrupt Republicans who steal money. He pardoned former Tennessee House Speaker Glen Casada and his chief of staff, Cade Cothren, who had been convicted of several charges of wire fraud and money laundering. Casada resigned as speaker after a scandal in which he and Cothren sent racist and sexist text messages. They had gone on to start a consulting firm together through which they funneled campaign and taxpayer money to themselves. They ripped off their own House Republicans, who'd thought they were hiring them to manage their political mailings. They had been investigated during Trump's first term and sentenced by a Trump-appointed judge. Still, the White House claimed that the convictions had been a political smear by the Biden team for "a minor issue involving constituent matters."

Then there's George Santos, the New York Republican congressman whose name isn't always George Santos, who served less than three months of a seven-year prison sentence for wire fraud and identity theft. The sentence included more than $370,000 in restitution that Santos was supposed to pay back to his victims, including two donors who had given him $25,000 each for TV ads to support his campaign. He spent the money on designer clothes and paying off his debts. He used other campaign funds for plastic surgery, trips to Atlantic City and Las Vegas, and subscriptions on OnlyFans. He was expelled from the Republican-controlled House of Representatives by a bipartisan majority of 311–114. His name is a stain on the Baruch

College volleyball team, which he led to four straight national titles, while also teaching himself French, Latin, Mandarin, and quantum computing.

Trump commuted his sentence to release him from prison immediately, with this astonishing explanation: "George Santos was somewhat of a 'rogue,' but there are many rogues throughout our Country that aren't forced to serve seven years in prison."

Ironically enough, a disproportionate number of those rogues can be found sitting on the undemolished side of the White House.

You might think that the House Republicans who expelled Santos from Congress would have voiced some muted displeasure at the freeing of someone the trial judge called "an arrogant fraudster." But no. The party of law and order, family values, and Christian nationalism rolled over and played dead. "The president has the right in the Constitution for pardon and commutation of course," said House Speaker Mike Johnson. "We believe in redemption. This is a personal belief of mine. And I hope Mr. Santos makes the most of his second chance."

Sadly, such personal beliefs are no match for the intentions of some of Trump's pardoned criminals. Jonathan Braun was originally sentenced to ten years in prison after pleading guilty to drug charges in 2019. He was a high-ranking member of an international group that smuggled more than 100,000 kilos (220,000 pounds) of marijuana from Canada into the United States. You know, the kind of thing that Trump now claims is a justification for slapping tariffs on Canada or blowing up a fishing boat in the Caribbean. Braun's sentence was commuted in the final days of Trump's first term, thanks to a family connection with Trump's son-in-law Jared Kushner.

Redemption was not on Braun's mind when prosecutors said he later sexually assaulted a nanny, swung an IV pole at a hospital nurse and threatened to kill her, and screamed at a congregant at his synagogue. Nor was he thinking about his second chance when prosecutors said he assaulted a three-year-old or when he loan-sharked small businesses. He was fined $20 million for predatory lending practices in 2024 and sentenced to twenty-seven months in prison in 2025.

Even more than the rank hypocrisy, there's a curious, repetitive pattern to Trump's pardons. It's almost as if he sees himself in the corrupt fraudsters who belong to his MAGA party and the criminals with connections to his inner circle.

At some point—and we are long past that point—the presidential power of the pardon undermines the rule of law that is the foundation of the United States. Trump's second term has turned the pardon into a get-out-of-jail-free card susceptible to the whims and crooked schemes of the president.

People in Washington often talk about a looming constitutional crisis if Trump ignores the courts or Congress or declares martial law. But his abuse of the presidential pardon power is already a constitutional crisis, as it pits one part of the Constitution against another. You cannot reconcile the rule of law with pardons that undermine that rule of law.

Nowhere is this more obvious than in Trump's pardons of those convicted for their activities on January 6, 2021, and regarding the 2020 election. That includes the insurrection on Capitol Hill, the fraudulent plan to submit fake electors' names, and the baseless legal challenges that smeared the reputations of voting machine companies and election officials. All of it represents an assault on democracy and the rule of law.

On his very first day back in the Oval Office, Trump granted clemency to nearly 1,600 people convicted of or indicted for crimes committed during the January 6 attack on the Capitol. Most of them received pardons. Some of them had their sentences commuted. Among them was Enrique Tarrio, the leader of the Proud Boys militia, serving a twenty-two-year sentence for organizing the sedition. There was also Alan Hostetter, a retired police chief who had driven to the nation's capital armed with hatchets, knives, and stun batons, along with a bullhorn that he used to encourage the insurrectionists to attack police officers. He had been sentenced to eleven years in prison.

The great crime-fighting president also granted clemency to David

Dempsey, who had been sentenced to twenty years in prison for stomping on the heads of police officers, as well as using flagpoles and pepper spray to attack them. He waved his kinglike mercy over Daniel Rodriguez, sentenced to twelve and a half years in prison for crimes including shooting an officer multiple times with a stun gun.

You get the picture. Trump could have taken the time to separate out the violent offenders from the nonviolent ones. That was what his own vice president expected. "If you committed violence on that day, obviously you shouldn't be pardoned," JD Vance told Fox News eight days before the violent thugs were pardoned. But separating out the bad from the evil would have taken too much work. "Fuck it, release 'em all," Trump told his aides, according to Axios. As part of his formal statement, he said that his pardons ended what he called "a grave national injustice that has been perpetrated upon the American people over the last four years."

For someone who campaigned alongside police officers and has been endorsed three times by the National Fraternal Order of Police, the pardons were obviously a little problematic. "I am a friend of police, more than any president who's ever been in this office," Trump said as he pardoned all the brutal thugs who had attacked the police. But he explained that the criminals themselves deserved their freedom. "Their lives have been ruined," he said. "They served years in jail. And if you look at the American public, the American public is tired of it."

In case there was any confusion about Trump's "Fuck it" mentality regarding democracy, he followed up with a slew of pardons ten months later. That round included the lawyers and cronies who had plotted, incompetently, to overturn the 2020 election results: Rudy Giuliani, John Eastman, and Sidney Powell, along with his former chief of staff Mark Meadows and his adviser Boris Epshteyn. The pardons extended to the gang of state officials who had submitted fake slates of electors to mess with the Electoral College and the official certification of the 2020 results.

The pardons were symbolic; none of his antidemocratic cronies were facing federal charges. In fact, some of them are still facing prosecution at the state level, where federal elections are actually managed and Trump's pardons have no impact. However, the symbolism speaks volumes about Trump's disrespect for democracy and the disastrously unchecked power of the pardon. White House Press Secretary Karoline Leavitt claimed that the pardons had somehow all been about defending our elections. "These great Americans were persecuted and put through hell by the Biden Administration for challenging an election, which is the cornerstone of democracy," she said.

For Karoline's sake, let's consider what actually happened surrounding that election. Trump's legal team filed more than sixty lawsuits contesting his defeat in 2020. They all failed, some of them at the hands of Trump-appointed judges. Except for one, which shortened a ballot cure deadline in Pennsylvania—a ruling that was duly reversed by the state's supreme court. Judges found them frivolous, without merit, lacking standing, or simply lacking evidence. Just like the fake electors, they were intended to muddy the waters, confuse the public, and interfere with a free and fair election. Those legal scams were the cornerstone of democracy as much as Trump's golden ballroom is the cornerstone of conservation.

On the very same day he pardoned his fake lawyers and fake electors, Trump also pardoned—for no good reason—a trail runner who had cheated in order to break a speed record of going up and down Grand Teton in Wyoming. Michelino Sunseri had been prosecuted for using a restricted trail that is meant to protect the national park from erosion. Trump loves nobody more than a fellow crook, no matter how big or small the crooked scheme.

* * *

There are two obstacles to reforming the unchecked power of the presidency. Neither is easy to overcome. But both are necessary if we're serious about saving our democracy. Because you can be sure that future presidents after Trump—Democrats and Republicans alike—will assert the same powers, with no checks and balances, unless we act to stop them in the first weeks and months of the next administration.

The first and biggest obstacle is the high bar for enacting a constitutional amendment. There's a reason why the last amendment was passed in 1992, and it was a minor one relating to the timing of pay increases or decreases for members of Congress. It took 202 years to be ratified after its initial proposal in 1789. Its intention was to reduce corruption, so that salary increases can happen only after an election. In practice, politicians have become much more skilled at engaging in corruption since the founding of the republic, especially during the Trump years.

A constitutional amendment needs two-thirds majorities in the House and Senate, and those aren't even the highest bars to cross. The far tougher requirement is ratification by three-fourths of the states. Before the Twenty-seventh Amendment, the Twenty-sixth, which lowered the voting age from twenty-one to eighteen, was ratified in 1971, when the nation agreed that if an eighteen-year-old American could be conscripted to die in Vietnam, he should also be given the right to vote.

The more immediate way to rebuild our democracy and the rule of law is through legislation by Congress. That was what happened in the years after Watergate, when Congress passed a series of laws to limit presidential power and increase transparency in government. The great post-Nixon reforms gave us an inspector general in each federal agency, internal watchdogs to investigate waste, fraud, and abuse. They were naturally one of the first targets of Trump's purges as soon as he got back into power.

Nixon's perversion of the presidency inspired Congress to pass the Ethics in Government Act of 1978, requiring financial disclosures of public officials, restricting lobbying, and creating the Office of Government Ethics to oversee the executive branch. Building on the Freedom of Information Act of 1966, which gave the public access to government records, there was the Presidential Records Act of 1978, designed to protect the kinds of papers that Trump was so desperate to hide in his bathroom at Mar-a-Lago.

Above all, Congress reasserted its own powers even before Nixon quit. In July 1974, it passed the Impoundment Control Act to stop presidents' refusing to spend funds directed by Congress, as Nixon had done and Trump would do again. In November 1973, it established the War Powers Resolution to require presidents to notify Congress within forty-eight hours of declaring hostilities against another nation and to seek congressional authorization for war within sixty days. Nixon vetoed the bill, but Congress overrode it. Trump chose to simply ignore it as he launched strikes on boats in the Caribbean and dropped thousands of bombs on Iran in an attempt to change the regime.

What's to stop a post-Trump Congress from passing a sweeping set of legal reforms to curb the imperial presidency and reestablish the checks and balances of the Constitution? The short answer is: the disastrous 2024 Supreme Court ruling in *Trump v. United States*. At the center of that case were the undisputed facts of Trump's very public attempts to overturn the election results of 2020, the ones that had officially declared him a loser. Trump had been indicted on four charges around his fake electors, pressuring his vice president, Mike Pence, to count the fake elector votes, pressuring state officials to "find" extra votes to hand him victory, and encouraging the riot at the Capitol on January 6, 2021.

The facts of Trump's scheming to overturn democracy have never been in serious dispute. Nevertheless, the Trump Supreme Court handed him—and all future presidents—the ultimate, and literal, get-out-of-jail-free card. In the summer of 2024, it ruled that there was absolute immunity from criminal prosecution for all the official acts of a president. There was also presumptive immunity for semi-official acts.

The Trump Supreme Court decided that Trump—and all future presidents—could act with impunity as long as they called whatever they did an official act. Even though the Constitution does not say anything about presidential immunity; even though the founders of the republic made it crystal clear that they wanted to avoid granting the president the absolute powers of a monarch. This is the same Trump Supreme Court that decided it could overturn *Roe v. Wade* because the Constitution does not explicitly talk about a right to privacy. Go figure.

As Justice Sotomayor wrote in the liberal dissent, the Court's ruling tore up the Constitution.

> Today's decision to grant former Presidents criminal immunity reshapes the institution of the Presidency. It makes a mockery of the principle, foundational to our Constitution and system of Government, that no man is above the law. . . .

> The President of the United States is the most powerful person in the country, and possibly the world. When he uses his official powers in any way, under the majority's reasoning, he now will be insulated from criminal prosecution. Orders the Navy's Seal Team 6 to assassinate a political rival? Immune. Organizes a military coup to hold onto power? Immune. Takes a bribe in exchange for a pardon? Immune. Immune, immune, immune. . . .

> Even if these nightmare scenarios never play out, and I pray they never do, the damage has been done. The relationship between the President and the people he serves has shifted irrevocably. In every use of official power, the President is now a king above the law.

Naturally, the liberal justices raised the question of a president ordering a political assassination. Naturally, the right-wing justices brushed aside that awkward objection, calling it "fear mongering on the basis of extreme hypotheticals."

It didn't take Trump a year in office to embrace most of the extreme hypotheticals. Extrajudicial killings in the Caribbean? Immune. Granting a pardon to a crypto billionaire, Changpeng Zhao, whose company invested billions of dollars in the Trump family business? Immune. Deploying the military to intimidate cities and states governed by political rivals? Immune.

* * *

So what does the day after Trump look like? First, the Supreme Court must be reformed, along with the Senate filibuster, or else nothing will change. Our democracy and the rule of law will continue to collapse.

To overturn the Trump Supreme Court's disastrous rulings, Congress needs to pass sweeping reform laws to restrict the unlimited powers and immunity of an imperial presidency. That would include the No Kings Act, proposed by dozens of Democratic senators, to make it clear that presidents do not have immunity for criminal actions. The legislation would remove the Supreme Court from being the appeals court on any criminal prosecution involving the president or vice president. That would instead be the responsibility of the United States Court of Appeals in Washington, DC.

With presidential immunity struck down, Congress can begin to limit the clear constitutional powers of the presidential pardon. For instance, Congress could make it a crime for the president to accept a bribe in exchange for a pardon. The pardon might stand, but a president—and the pardoned person—would face criminal charges. Congress could make it a criminal offense to use a pardon to undermine judicial proceedings or the administration of an election. And Congress should explicitly prohibit any attempt by any president to pardon him- or herself so as to avoid criminal prosecution.

None of these steps will be easy. They are all disruptive. They all require the courage of our elected officials, whose job it is to rebuild our democracy and the rule of law. But it wasn't easy to rebuild after Nixon and Watergate. It wasn't easy to rebuild after the Civil War. Standing up for democracy is no job for the fainthearted. Yet it's a job that American voters are crying out for. Public trust in government is at historic lows, with just one in five Americans saying that their government does what's right always or most of the time. Back in the 1960s, that number was close to four in five Americans.

Cleaning up our politics—restoring trust in government—has to start at the top. It's time to reform the powers of the presidency—before it's too late and we have no power to rein in the king.

7

The Con in the Economy

Donald Trump knows a thing or two about the art of the con. After all those years in real estate and reality TV, the formula is as simple as he is: Project supreme confidence, tell the suckers they're getting a deal, and lie about the results.

This playbook has worked best on the single most important issue to voters: the economy. With zero experience of holding elected office or even running a major corporation, Trump's only pitch for the presidency in 2016 was his supposed mastery of business. Granted, we're talking about a family business that declared bankruptcy no fewer than six times. But that didn't stop him from projecting the appearance of wealth, bolstered by his performance on *The Apprentice*.

Here's how Trump sold himself to a gullible public in his first TV debate with Hillary Clinton in 2016. When asked about why he wasn't releasing his tax returns, he moaned about being audited and then boasted about declaring—on another financial statement—income of $694 million. "If you would have told me I was going to make that fifteen or twenty years ago, I would have been very surprised," he said modestly. "But that's the kind of thinking that our country needs. When we have a country that's doing so badly, that's being ripped off by every single country in the world, it's the kind of thinking that our country needs, because everybody . . . we have a trade deficit with all of the countries that we do business with, of almost $800 billion a year. You know what that is? That means, who's negotiating these trade deals? We have people that are political hacks negotiating our trade deals."

Talk about magical thinking. There's no connection between his stated income and "the kind of thinking that our country needs." There's even less of a connection between our trade deficit and the country being ripped off. In fact, the trade deficit is the result of American consumers' buying cheap stuff from low-wage countries—which, if anything, amounts to our ripping off those countries' workers. But none of that purported economic brainpower matters, because the only important line is the one Trump continues to peddle to this day: that he can negotiate trade deals better than political hacks. And if he can negotiate a better trade deal, maybe you, too, could enjoy an income that you couldn't even imagine fifteen or twenty years ago.

The truth is that if he actually lived up to his own hype, he wouldn't need to undermine our elections because he would handily win every one. The economy would be so rosy that his popularity would be through the roof—in real polls, not imaginary ones. Instead, the harsh economic reality of Trump's con is the direct cause of his desperate need to destroy our democracy.

Here's the factual reality of Trump's first term: Over the course of his four years in office, the number of jobs declined by half a percentage point. Under eight years of Barack Obama, they grew by 1 point, and under four years of Joe Biden, they grew by 2.7 points.

Trump claims that his economy was doing great until the covid pandemic struck in his final year in office, as if other presidents had it easy. As if Obama had been handed a stellar economy after the financial meltdown and Great Recession of 2008. As if the pandemic had been over when Biden entered the Oval Office in 2021.

But let's grant him covid. Trump's numbers are actually *worse* if you just look at his first year in office in his first term. The economy was growing at an annual rate of around 1.5 percent when he entered the White House in 2017. One year later, it was less than 0.5 percent. By any measure, Trump has the worst economic record of any president—Republican or Democrat—since the Great Depression of the 1930s.

All those Trump voters should not be surprised at the dismal economy of his second term. They may have thought that they were voting for a president who would usher in an economic boom. But the economy in 2025 was growing at 2 percent, compared to almost 3 percent in Biden's final years. Job growth in Biden's final year averaged 186,000 a month. In Trump's first six months, it was 40 percent lower. By the summer, it cratered 80 percent lower.

You don't have to be a professional pollster to know why Republicans have lost their polling advantage on the economy. In 2023, they led Democrats by 12 points on the economy. In 2025, that lead shrank to just 3 points. Even Republicans have soured on the second Trump economy: Just 44 percent of Republicans say that the economy is either excellent or good compared with 81 percent in Trump's first term, before the pandemic.

In fairness, Trump is not the only Republican president to whiff at economic revitalization. Under George W. Bush, the number of jobs barely grew at all during his eight years in office, rising by just 0.13 percent. The economy grew in Bush's first year at less than 2 percent, a relatively low rate not seen since Jimmy Carter's first year in office.

This economic con extends well beyond the huckster currently sitting in the Oval Office. It's a Republican charade that has persisted for decades. Republicans may be in bed with big business. They may be funded by some of the wealthiest Americans in the country. But none of that means that their economic policies are successful. Their real achievement is not helping families achieve their American dream; it's bamboozling voters into thinking that they're any good at managing the economy for anyone not in Trump's tax bracket.

Don't take my word for it. Two economics professors at Princeton

University, Alan Blinder and Mark Watson, studied the numbers. They found that by every major indicator—employment, GDP growth, incomes, even the stock market—the economy has grown much faster under Democratic presidents than Republicans. In fact, they found the annual average rate of economic growth under Democratic presidents to be almost double the rate under Republicans. That's dating back as far as the data goes, to 1933. The six presidents with the fastest job growth are all Democrats. Ronald Reagan is the most recent Republican with an economic record that compares with that of Democratic presidents. He left the White House almost half a century ago.

If the study did not stretch so far back, you could brush it all away as a fluke—or a case of confusion, because of the role Congress plays in taxation and spending. But you can't, because the data is so consistent. The only real explanation is that Democrats have followed the facts and the numbers to shape economies that work for most Americans, while Republicans have clung to their fantasies that tax cuts for the rich will trickle down and that less regulation of big business will be good for everyone.

You can fool all of the people only some of the time. Eventually, they cotton on to every con man. Trump can pretend that the economy is going like gangbusters—or fire the people in charge of the numbers—but everyday Americans have their own data on the economy. It's called their wallets. Inflation in Trump's first year back was 3.0 percent, a slight rise from 2.9 percent in Biden's last year. Economic confidence, according to Gallup, was –14 in 2025, when America was supposed to be great all over again. That's pretty much where it was in Biden's first year in office. It was around +20 when Obama left the White House.

After Democrats swept the off-year elections in Virginia and New Jersey in 2025, Trump could not avoid the media questions about his own dismal economy. "The affordability is much better with the Republicans," he said. "The only problem is the Republicans don't talk about it, and Republicans should start talking about it and use their heads."

How should Republicans talk about the cost of living that remains as stubbornly high as Trump's self-esteem? "I think polls are fake," he told Fox News. "We have the greatest economy we've ever had." Well, then, that settles it.

All this talk about affordability is a bunch of Democratic lies, according to the most honest president America never had. "Affordability is a lie when used by the Dems," he posted on the platform he laughably calls Truth Social. "It is a complete CON JOB."

Putting the con back into the economy. It's all Trump really knows about the subject.

* * *

Trump has long pretended to be the candidate of working Americans. After he won the presidency the first time around, he read out loud some words he obviously didn't have any hand in writing: He promised to be a president for all Americans; that he would seek common ground with the rest of the world. He would never come close to saying that again—except for one line that lies at the heart of his supposedly populist politics, about standing up for the little guy against all those crooked elites. "The forgotten men and women of our country will be forgotten no longer," he declared in his victory speech in New York in November 2016.

Trump sells a lot of his policy ideas as things that will help the little guy. Kicking out immigrants, for instance. That's going to help the little guy, who will soon be free to do all those stolen jobs such as harvesting strawberries in the blistering sun for $1.20 per case.

The little guy will finally feel safer without all those immigrants around, what with their criminal insanity and all. "We have millions of people pouring into our country from prisons and jails, from mental institutions and insane asylums," he said in his TV debate with Kamala Harris in September 2024, clearly betraying his confusion between insane asylums and *claiming* asylum. "And they're coming in and they're taking jobs that are occupied right now by African

Americans and Hispanics and also unions. Unions are going to be affected very soon."

If there's any consistency to this nonsense, it's this: He returns time and again to the political bromide that he's helping the working folks of America. "Every policy of the Trump administration is designed to lift up the American worker, promote great-paying blue-collar jobs, and to rebuild the industrial bedrock of our nation," he told his cabinet before Labor Day in his first year back in the White House. ". . . You're going to see the new job numbers are going to be through the roof because of all of the different businesses that are moving into our country," he continued. "And not just production businesses, autos and AI, but any business you can think of."

Every policy for the workers! Jobs for everyone! In any business you can think of!

Trump has done just enough to pretend to care about working Americans but not nearly enough to help the little guy in reality. As the presidential election year began in 2024, he met with the leaders of the Teamsters Union to try to peel its members away from the Democrats. Union members in general favor Democrats: Joe Biden won 56 percent of union members and households in 2020. But the Teamsters are different. They were famously investigated by Congress and the federal government in the 1950s and 1960s for corruption and infiltration by organized crime. They supported Reagan and Bush in the 1980s, although they leaned toward Democrats in the 1990s. Polls in 2024 showed 60 percent of Teamsters members supporting Trump over Harris. Trump asked the Teamsters leadership to support his campaign. "Usually a Republican wouldn't get that endorsement," he said after meeting them in early 2024. ". . . But in my case it's different because I've employed thousands of Teamsters and I thought we should come over and pay our respects. And as you know, a big part of the voting bloc votes for me."

The meeting came after the union president, Sean O'Brien, traveled to Mar-a-Lago to meet privately with Trump. They posed for a photo afterward, both of them flashing their thumbs up. Sure enough, O'Brien traveled to Milwaukee to speak at the opening night of the Republican National Convention in the summer of 2024. "At the end of the day, the Teamsters are not interested if you have a D, R, or an I next to your name," he said. "We want to know one thing: What are you doing to help American workers?"

Here's what Trump did to help American workers in his first term: He cut corporate income tax rates, which overwhelmingly helped the top 1 percent of the country. As he told his dinner guests at Mar-a-Lago at the time, "You all just got a lot richer." He opposed a Labor Department rule that gave overtime protection to 12.5 million workers. He weakened protections for tipped workers, allowing employers to pocket their tips if they paid their employees the minimum wage. He supported companies forcing their employees to sign arbitration agreements so they couldn't file class action lawsuits. He even blocked regulations to protect fair pay and workplace safety. The Teamsters rewarded him by refusing to endorse Kamala Harris. They instead endorsed no candidate, for the first time since the 1990s.

Here's how Trump repaid the support of working-class voters and persuadable union leaders such as the Teamsters president. In his first hundred days, he allowed Elon Musk and his so-called Department of Government Efficiency to fire around 300,000 federal workers in a process that was so chaotic that they had to rehire thousands of people they had just fired. They gutted the National Institute for Occupational Safety and Health, which is responsible for workers' health and safety standards. They also canceled grants for programs to combat forced and child labor around the world, which is supposed to protect American workers from unfair competition. There were even orders to reduce the minimum wage for federal contractors.

On January 28, 2025, Trump weakened the National Labor Relations Board by firing its acting chair, Gwynne Wilcox, and its general counsel, Jennifer Abruzzo. His email ordering their termination didn't even pretend to stand up for the forgotten men and women of America. "Viewing their record collectively, I lack confidence that Commissioners Wilcox and General Counsel Abruzzo can fairly evaluate matters before them without unduly disfavoring the interests of employers large and small," he wrote.

That is the first-year record of a president who pretends that every one of his policies is designed to lift up American workers. He canceled $5 billion under the bipartisan infrastructure law passed in 2021 to create a national network of electric vehicle charging stations. That cancellation was illegal, according to the nonpartisan Government Accountability Office. But it still killed thousands of jobs. He even stopped the construction of a wind farm off the coast of Rhode Island that was 80 percent complete. That left several hundred workers literally out at sea.

More than anything else, Trump showed where his economic priorities lie with the monstrous tax and spending bill that he liked to call big and beautiful. They did not lie with the forgotten men and women of America or the health of the American economy. For context, Trump's landmark legislation will cost $3.4 trillion over the next ten years, mostly due to his giant tax cuts. It dwarfs Biden's biggest new spending bills, including his covid stimulus package and the bipartisan infrastructure law.

How does the bill help the little guy? It doesn't. According to the Congressional Budget Office, the highest 10 percent of earners will see their incomes rise by 2.7 percent over the next decade, thanks to the tax cuts. The lowest 10 percent of American earners will see their incomes *fall* by 3.1 percent because of sweeping cuts to Medicaid and food stamps. "It is the largest wealth transfer in American history," said Senator Brian Schatz from Hawaii. "They're literally taking from the poor—people who don't have enough money—and shoveling straight into the pockets of people who already have more than enough. This bill is about making the richest people to ever walk the earth even richer."

As it happens, Trump couldn't even fool all the people for some of the time about his massive tax cuts for the rich. Polls showed 61 percent of Americans opposing the bill, with only 29 percent saying it would help the economy. Even a good chunk of people supporting the bill thought it wouldn't make much difference. By the fall, just a couple of months after signing the monstrosity into law, Trump's team was telling Republicans to stop calling it the One Big Beautiful Bill, as they had all along. Instead, they needed to call it the Working Families Tax Cut Bill. Because it obviously wasn't.

What about Trump's appeal to tipped workers by giving them tax deductions? Surely that helps the forgotten men and women. As it happens, the tax deductions for tips are capped at $25,000, and they expire in three years—coinciding with the time when Trump leaves office, and he can no longer take credit, so why bother? Besides, one-third of tipped workers earn so little that they pay no federal income tax at all, according to researchers at the Brookings Institution. On top of that, tipped workers in restaurants do not include the people who cook the food or clean the floors. And tipped workers experience high rates of wage theft by unscrupulous employers, who will no doubt use the tax breaks to keep their base wages lower than ever.

But all of that pales in comparison to the unpopularity of Trump's crown jewel: his tariffs. The clear majority of Americans—61 percent in a recent Pew Research Center poll—disapprove of the economic policy that Trump is proudest of. Even though it's totally illegal for him to slap tariffs on countries around the world without a vote in Congress; and even though Trump keeps telling the American people that other countries are paying the tariffs. The forgotten men and women of America simply don't approve.

Here's what's going on in the real world: American consumers are paying for those tariffs in the form of higher prices. Like any other sales tax, they hit lower-income households harder than wealthy ones. Tariffs are regressive because working Americans spend more of their income on buying goods and services than the rich do. They are the ones hit by higher prices on cheap imports on Amazon or at Walmart. On top of higher taxes, the tariffs don't even work as Trump has always promised they would. They aren't forcing companies to create manufacturing jobs in the United States. Big corporations either are shuffling their supply chains to other countries that have negotiated lower tariffs or are passing on those tax hikes to their customers by charging higher prices. In fact, research by the San Francisco Federal Reserve into 150 years of tariffs in the United States and around the world found that tariffs depress economies and drive unemployment higher. That might just explain why manufacturing lost 42,000 jobs in the four months after Trump touted his Liberation Day tariffs. That came after Trump had promised a manufacturing renaissance.

The truth is that every con ends the same way: The huckster gets rumbled by the mob. They chase him out of town, and he rolls on to the next stop, where the con can begin again. If the tax cuts and the tariffs don't shatter the con, Trump's embrace of AI surely will. In the summer of his first year back in power, he spoke at a conference called "Winning the AI Race." "America is the country that started the AI race. And as president of the United States, I'm here today to declare that America is going to win it," he said. "So from this day forward, it'll be the policy of the United States to do whatever it takes to lead the world in artificial intelligence. Such an important thing happening. This is really something that nobody expected. It just popped out of the air and here we are."

So many things just pop out of the air inside Trump's head. Like his embrace of AI, which his onetime political guru Steve Bannon thinks is a disaster. Bannon may be nuts, but he believes that middle-class jobs "are going to be eviscerated" by AI—and that AI will be front and center in the 2028 election. This isn't some genius insight. Dario Amodei, the cofounder and CEO of Anthropic, said that AI could wipe out half of all entry-level white-collar jobs in the next few years, driving unemployment to between 10 and 20 percent. At the worst point of the Great Recession in 2009, unemployment hit 10 percent. It reached 25 percent at the worst point of the Great Depression in 1933.

This may not be a problem for Trump himself, whose crypto fortune and old age mean that he'll never have to experience an AI workplace. But it will be a problem for his vice president, JD Vance, when he campaigns in 2028. "We will always center American workers in our AI policy," Vance said in his first month on the job at the Artificial Intelligence Action Summit in Paris. "We refuse to view AI as a purely disruptive technology that will inevitably automate away our labor force. We believe and we will fight for policies that ensure that AI is going to make our workers more productive, and we expect that they will reap the rewards with higher wages, better benefits, and safer and more prosperous communities."

These are the kinds of promises that come back to haunt presidential candidates in thirty-second attack ads. Because they are plainly not true—like all the other cons in the Trump economy.

* * *

Let's face it, economic statistics can be hard to understand. So what's the easiest way to know that the Trump economy isn't working for working Americans? By looking at Trump himself. If the Trump economy benefits anyone, it's the man sitting in the Oval Office, who is concerned with one person and one person only, not the forgotten men and women of America.

Tariffs are the centerpiece of Trump's economic policies, and they just happen to represent some of the clearest evidence of his corruption. Take the case of Switzerland, which managed to convince him to cut tariffs on its goods from 39 to 15 percent. This is how the country did it: by giving him a 1-kilogram (2.2-pound) gold bar stamped with the numbers 45 and 47 in homage to Trump's presidencies. The value of the gold is more than $130,000. White House officials claim that the transaction was legal because Trump accepted the gift on behalf of his presidential library. Besides, the Supreme Court ruled that he can't face criminal prosecution for any official act. There's a reason why economists say that tariffs encourage corruption around the world.

Trump happily accepted the gold bar—along with a golden Rolex desktop clock—just a few months after Bob Menendez, a former New Jersey senator, was sentenced to eleven years in prison for bribery. Menendez was jailed and disgraced for doing political favors in exchange for expensive gifts. Among those bribes were gold bars, one of which was passed to the jurors during his trial.

I know this thought experiment is familiar, but it's worth repeating: Can you imagine—for a second—any Democratic president doing something similar and staying in office? If Barack Obama had accepted a solid gold bar from a foreign country in exchange for changing US policy, he would have been impeached and convicted within weeks—not just by every single Republican but also by a majority of Democrats.

Somehow Trump is widely credited with understanding the mindset of working Americans. But he just accepted a gold bar worth more than twice what a regular full-time worker earns in a whole year in this country. And it wasn't even headline news.

For Senator Elizabeth Warren, a Massachusetts Democrat, fighting corruption is central to restoring our democracy. "It's impossible to overstate the importance of beating corruption out of the system in Washington, because it's the key to unlocking every other thing we want to do. Why do we not have sensible gun legislation? Because of corruption. Why do we not pass laws that make prescription drugs more affordable, something that ninety percent of Americans want to see us do? Because of corruption," she told me. "It's impossible for anyone, Democrat or Republican, to escape the underlying reality that this is a presidency for sale. We were having problems with corruption long before Donald Trump became president. The problem was getting worse and worse, but Donald Trump has taken corruption into hyperspace."

Trump's claim to economic expertise lies at the heart of the MAGA pitch to voters. If Democrats are going to save our democracy and rebuild this country after Trump leaves office, they need to attack that economic pitch. One of the ways to do that is to talk a lot, as New

York mayor Zohran Mamdani did during his campaign, about the cost of living. That remains the single most important issue for voters in poll after poll after poll.

The other approach is to target the corruption at the heart of MAGA power. Voters do not distinguish between their feelings of disgust for corruption in both parties. But they do understand that there is an urgent need for reform.

Polling by Navigator Research tested two messages against the classic Trump trope that everybody is corrupt. One message was about the unprecedented nature of Trump's corruption: "The scale of corruption under Trump massively outweighs that of any past presidency, Democrat or Republican, and we need to do something about it." The other was about the need for major reform: "Washington has a major corruption problem in both parties, and we need to enact significant reforms and overhaul the system to hold Trump, as well as other Republicans and Democrats, accountable for corruption." The anti-Trump message beat the Republican trope by 13 points. But the reform message dominated the Republican trope by 41 points. Trump's corruption is a chance for a pitch to the American people that is centered on reform.

Economic reform goes well beyond the corruption of elected officials. It gets to the heart of an economic system that is skewed to benefit big corporations and the ultrawealthy. The most immediate way to level the playing field is to correct the Trump tax giveaways. Raising taxes on big businesses and the wealthy is an overwhelmingly popular idea among American voters. A clear majority—63 percent, including 43 percent of Republicans—is in favor of raising taxes on big corporations. A similar-sized majority—58 percent—is in favor of raising taxes on households earning more than $400,000 a year, which is more than four times the median income. Once again, that support includes 43 percent of Republicans, according to polling by the Pew Research Center.

Since the 1990s shift to the centrist politics of the "third way,"

Democrats have shied away from this kind of economic populism. Those days are surely over. Raising taxes on big corporations and wealthy households has clear majority support across the country. Democrats need to lose their fear about interfering with business or alienating middle-class voters. If you're earning more than $400,000, you don't represent the mainstream middle class, where elections are won and lost.

Beating MAGA populists means challenging them on their own concocted claim to care about the forgotten people. If Democrats want to appeal to working-class voters, they need to champion raising the federal minimum wage, which stands at just $7.25 an hour. It hasn't changed since 2009. Dozens of states have their own minimum-wage levels that are far higher, including the battleground states of Ohio, Michigan, and Arizona. Even Trump's home state of Florida vastly outstrips the federal minimum at $14 an hour.

In the middle of the pandemic, the Congressional Budget Office examined the effects of raising the federal minimum wage to $15 an hour. It found that it would help 17 million Americans, lifting 900,000 out of poverty. At the time, opinion polls found that 62 percent of voters agreed with raising the minimum wage to $15. The Biden administration failed to do so at the time because of the Senate filibuster rules—and because the Senate parliamentarian ruled that the minimum wage did not meet the budget rules to bypass the filibuster. Of course, the administration wasn't helped by its own Arizona Democrat, Kyrsten Sinema, rejecting a minimum-wage hike with a curtsy on the Senate floor during the votes on the pandemic relief bill.

That's no reason to give up. In fact, it's every reason to campaign on an economic agenda that raises the minimum wage. If you're worried about Trump's appeal to tipped workers, why not raise their minimum wage? It stands at a miserable $2.13 an hour. Polling shows that 81 percent of Americans believe that tipped workers should get the same minimum wage as everyone else does.

Trump's economic populism isn't just a con; it's a massive political opportunity for progressives. It opens the door to vote-winning campaigns and life-changing policies. If we're serious about saving our democracy and rebuilding the country the day after Trump leaves the White House, the next president's agenda must start with pocketbook issues. After all these years, and after all the political turmoil, it's still the economy, stupid.

8

Live and Let Die

There's only one thing that gets under the thin skin of Donald Trump more than the fact that he lost the 2020 election. That's Barack Obama. Aside from the obvious factors—such as his intelligence, his charisma, and, naturally, the color of his skin—there's the truly annoying matter of 44's enduring popularity. Obama won two elections by margins that were far bigger than Trump's victories. He continues to have a favorability rating about 20 points higher than Trump's, according to Gallup. And let's not forget that he cracked those killer jokes about Trump in front of all those snickering White House correspondents. The whole room laughed at the reality TV star instead of taking him seriously as he tried to smear Obama about his birth certificate.

Any reminder of Obama pains Trump more than most of his many failures. And there is no greater reminder of his popular predecessor than Obamacare's tenacious grip on American life. Trump has talked repeatedly about replacing or repealing the landmark legislation of the Obama presidency, officially known as the Affordable Care Act. He even came close to making his anti-Obama dreams come true in 2017, with the so-called American Health Care Act.

With complete control of Washington, Trump and his MAGA party concocted a plan that destroyed the requirement that everyone must buy medical insurance—known as the individual mandate—which helps spread the cost of insurance across all Americans. Without it, Obamacare would be fatally weakened and premiums would spike for everyone. The plan also slashed Medicaid benefits for low-income Americans and messed with the rules that force insurers to cover preexisting conditions. It was, by any measure, a disastrous law that would reduce health care coverage, raise costs, and drive more Americans to risk living without medical insurance. It could even lead to death spirals for insurers as their business models fall apart. By 2026, Trump's proposed law was forecast to push 24 million Americans off of medical insurance.

After all the chest thumping about the evils of Obamacare, you'd think that the GOP would have readied a better plan. But no. Trump had campaigned on promising "affordable coverage for everyone"—probably because it sounded good. The reality is that Obamacare was, in fact, a Republican plan to begin with. And not just any old Republican plan; it had begun life as a set of ideas from the Heritage Foundation—yes, the one behind Project 2025—some of which were even more of an imposition on employers than Obamacare was.

You see, the GOP was caught in its own death spiral. By political preference, they should have left Obamacare alone. Due to their personal hatred, they needed to destroy it.

So the Obamacare replacement scraped through the House by a margin of just four votes, with twenty Republicans voting against it. It landed in the Senate on life support, where it turned into a hobbled version that took a more careful approach to gutting Americans' health insurance. All that was needed was fifty votes to crush the biggest legislative achievement of Obama's presidency—and with it his legacy. The prospects were promising. Republicans had bypassed the filibuster by pretending that the bill was about the budget, not just their oldest beef with Obama. With a 50–50 tie, they could count on Vice President Mike Pence to win the day. Instead, when push came to shove, three Republicans voted it down: Susan Collins of Maine, Lisa Murkowski of Alaska, and John McCain of Arizona. McCain was the last vote, pointing his thumb down like an emperor ordering the death of a gladiator.

Trump never forgot or forgave him for that. Even after McCain passed away, Trump couldn't let it go. "I never was a fan of John McCain, and I never will be," he said in the Oval Office. "Our country would have saved a trillion dollars, and we would have had great health care."

Yeah, right. The Congressional Budget Office forecast that the Republican bill would save just $150 billion over a decade. Premiums would have spiked for older Americans. And of course, millions of people would have lost coverage altogether. It was a disaster as health care policy. It was also a disaster as electoral politics. There's good reason to think that all those Republicans' votes to ruin American health care were a big factor in their heavy losses in the midterm elections the following year, when Democrats took back the House by the biggest margin in modern American history.

Trump didn't learn his lesson the second time around. (He tends not to.) With no actual health care plan or policy—not even an ideological direction that made any sense—the MAGA mob looked at the health of Americans in 2025 as just another way to save money. That's because Trump wanted his "one big beautiful bill" so badly—a bill that was especially big in the way it blew up the entire federal budget with tax cuts for the rich and large corporations. Trump ended up cutting Medicaid for low-income Americans by 12 percent, while adding work requirements to make it harder to be eligible for benefits. He threw up new barriers and rules to make it harder to sign up for Obamacare plans. He even cut federal support for medical student loans, making life harder for the next generation of doctors.

It's a weird set of choices for someone who promised to make America affordable again. True, there are a lot of weird things that Trump does every day. But you don't need a degree from the University of

Pennsylvania's Wharton School of Business to know that rising health care costs are a big reason why Americans are struggling to afford a middle-class life. Over the last two decades, total spending on medical care has more than tripled. One out of every five dollars spent in the United States is spent on health care. Guess how the country pays for all those rising health care bills? Out-of-pocket annual costs have spiked from $970 per person when Obamacare was passed in 2010 to more than $1,500 in 2024. Almost half of Americans say that it's hard to afford health care, according to research by the KFF health policy group. Most of those live in households making less than $90,000 a year.

That's how we got to the point of the longest government shutdown in US history—because Americans' medical care is getting worse while costing more and Trump is making our national sickness even more life threatening. In the first four months after Trump signed his tax monster into law, hospitals and clinics across the country closed or limited services. Researchers estimated that more than three hundred rural hospitals were at risk of closing or cutting services. Among them was an obstetrics ward in rural Lavonia, Georgia, whose closure forced pregnant women to travel an hour to find care. In Maine, eighteen family planning clinics stopped offering primary care. In Virginia's Shenandoah Valley, three primary care clinics shut down.

When the shutdown loomed in late 2025, Democrats chose to make health care costs their last stand. Overall, the shutdown was triggered by a much bigger clash over Trump's destruction of entire departments and agencies, as well as his power grab from Congress on taxes and spending. But Democrats wanted to negotiate a deal to extend medical insurance subsidies to keep premiums down for about 20 million Americans on Obamacare policies. Without those subsidies, the annual premium for the average household would more than double, from $888 to $1,904, according to KFF estimates. Higher premiums drive people to drop out of coverage, increasing insurance costs for everyone else and shifting more costs to emergency rooms in public hospitals, for which state taxpayers end up paying even more.

In the end, the Democrats folded without any deal to extend the subsidies. As for the man who blew up American health care to cut taxes for the rich, he spat out a brand-new exceptional idea: to send money directly to Americans so they could "PURCHASE THEIR OWN, MUCH BETTER, HEALTHCARE." As it happens, posting in ALL CAPS on Truth Social doesn't constitute a health care policy— even though Lindsey Graham, the senator for South Carolina, called the idea "simply brilliant."

Simple, yes. Brilliant, not so much. If Trump sent every penny of the $35 billion in insurance subsidies to every taxpayer in the country, we would each receive around $200. That ought to do the trick. "The only healthcare I will support or approve is sending the money directly back to the people," Trump declared on Truth Social as senators despaired of coming to any kind of deal after the shutdown ended.

In other words, Trump's health care solution is another round of tax cuts. When you're a hammer, everything looks like a nail. When you're Donald Trump, you think you can buy off everyone.

His goofy vice president was left making empty promises about a great health care plan coming right around the corner. "People come to the president and say, 'No, no, no, don't talk about health care. That's a graveyard for Republicans. Republicans always lose on health care,'" JD Vance told Breitbart in November 2025. "And the president's like 'I don't care about the politics of it. This system is screwed up for the American people. We need to fix it. So let's go and do it. Politics be damned.'"

Ah, yes. Such a great American, our nonpolitical president. So bravely fighting for Americans' health care. By cutting their health care to give tax breaks to the rich.

* * *

Health care is as fundamental to the health of our democracy as it is to our own bodies. It's why economists analyze the state of countries by examining statistics such as life expectancy, childhood diseases, and maternal health. It's the measure of who we are as a country and whether our government successfully serves the people—or just the interests of the rich and powerful.

By these standards, the United States is failing badly. We spend far more per person on medical care than any other comparable country does. In fact, we spend more than 40 percent over and above the next big spender, Switzerland. We spend 85 percent more than Canada and more than twice as much as Japan. And it's getting worse. Over the last five decades, the gap between what we spend is growing, not shrinking, compared to other wealthy countries, according to KFF.

Maybe that wouldn't matter if we got the best health care in the world and we were the healthiest people in the world. Instead, the United States ranks last among wealthy countries on all the key measures of health: acute illnesses, chronic diseases, life expectancy, rates of death. Our country had the highest rate of excess deaths from covid-19 for people younger than seventy-five, according to research by the Commonwealth Fund.

When our democracy fails, so does our health. That might sound dramatic, but it's true, especially if you look at what happened after the Trump Supreme Court overturned *Roe v. Wade* to allow states to trample on women's fundamental right to control their own health. To be clear, at least two Trump-appointed justices, along with the Bush-appointed chief justice, misled the Senate about their view of the landmark abortion rights case during their confirmation hearings. Brett Kavanaugh had called it an "important precedent of the Supreme Court that has been reaffirmed many times." Neil Gorsuch had said much the same, adding "Once a case is settled, that adds to the determinacy of the law. What was once a hotly contested issue is no longer a hotly contested issue. We move forward." Then there's John Roberts, the chief justice, who had said that overruling a precedent such as *Roe* would be "a jolt to the legal system" because "precedent plays an important role in promoting stability and evenhandedness." This is what happens when democracy is undermined by ideologues who game the system to gain power.

Tierra Walker knew that her pregnancy could threaten her life. During her last pregnancy, she had developed preeclampsia and her twins had been stillborn. In the fall of 2024, she was pregnant again and suffering from high blood pressure and diabetes. She was worried about developing preeclampsia and what would happen to her fourteen-year-old son if she died. So she asked her doctor at Methodist Hospital Northeast near San Antonio if it would be better not to go ahead with the pregnancy. Her doctor said that there was no emergency; nothing was wrong with her pregnancy except for her own health. Two months later, her teenage son found her lifeless in bed. The thirty-seven-year-old dental assistant had died of preeclampsia at the twenty-week stage of her pregnancy.

Texas is one of twelve states with a total abortion ban. There's supposed to be an exception for what is called "a life-threatening medical emergency." But doctors and lawyers say that the exception is too narrow and too vague—and the penalties are too severe—to save lives. The punishment for doctors who violate the abortion ban in Texas is up to ninety-nine years in prison. The reality is that women with existing health conditions, such as Tierra, are not considered at risk even though their pregnancies are high risk. The risks the doctors prioritize are the ones they will face themselves if they break the laws banning abortion.

So many women were dying in childbirth that the conservative Texas Legislature was forced to pass a law in 2025 to clarify its own ban. But even minor changes are hard to make. Antiabortion activists oppose any exemptions for the life of the mother because they think that saving a woman's life is a slippery slope. It's not just in Texas; in other states with total bans, the same arguments have been used, as if the life of a mother is just a political game. The new Texas law says that the exception to the abortion ban still needs to be "life-threatening" but does not need to be "imminent." Doctors and lawyers believe that that clarification won't save lives because they can't prove that a life-threatening risk is certain—until it's too late.

That's the problem when the government tries to get between patients and doctors. It has no clue how to limit its own powers. Above all, it has no right to determine the most difficult decisions a patient needs to make.

Conservatives like to pretend that they support limited government and individual liberty. That's true unless it involves a woman's reproductive health, in which case those principles—as well as legal precedents—mean nothing. Their power grab, through the Supreme Court, has reshaped health care across the country for pregnant women. There are now maternity care deserts, where there are no obstetric providers or clinics providing maternity care, in 35 percent of counties, according to the Commonwealth Fund. Naturally, the states with abortion bans have fewer maternity care providers, and there are fewer medical students applying for ob-gyn residencies.

Guess what happens to maternal mortality in states with strict limits on abortion? It is 51 percent higher than in other states, according to researchers at Tulane University. In California and Massachusetts, for instance, there are pregnancy-related deaths of less than 25 per 100,000. Across the Deep South, the rate is at least twice as high.

That's on top of an already abysmal record of maternal health in the United States when compared to other high-income countries. The World Health Organization found that we are one of only seven countries in which maternal mortality is rising, at a time when it's declining around the world. The other countries include Venezuela, Mauritius, and Belize. There are 22 maternal deaths for every 100,000 live births in this country, compared to 5.5 in the United Kingdom, 3.5 in Germany, and zero in Norway. Among Black women, the rate is 49.5 maternal deaths. It's no coincidence that the United States is the only wealthy country with no requirement for paid maternity leave; in Norway, employers must provide forty-nine weeks of fully paid parental leave to care for young children.

The damage to our health is not confined to reproductive rights. When the Trump White House unconstitutionally usurped budget power from the Congress, it wiped out around $3 billion in science funding for the National Institutes of Health and the National Science Foundation. Those budget cuts didn't just trample over the law; they were ideologically driven, based on politics, prejudice, and downright ignorance. They targeted anything related to the environment. They targeted anything that smelled of diversity, equity, and inclusion. That included, bizarrely, a grant to investigate how neurons regulate immune cells in the retina, simply because the grant mentioned that the cells exhibit "diversity."

The Trump Supreme Court naturally sided with the cuts, even though Chief Justice John Roberts voted with the liberal justices to restore them. After all, they had been restored by a conservative judge in a lower court already. Judge William Young of Massachusetts, a Reagan appointee, had said that the cuts were clearly illegal. In a case regarding cuts in funding for research related to racial minorities and LGBTQ people, he said, "This represents racial discrimination and discrimination against America's LGBTQ community. . . . I would be blind not to call it out. My duty is to call it out."

* * *

Above all, Trump wanted to target everything related to vaccines and public health, as if his revenge tour for his defeat in 2020 should include anything that had pulled the nation out of the pandemic. His antiscience vendetta has been championed by his unhinged health secretary, Robert F. Kennedy, Jr. A longtime antiscience buffoon, RFK Jr. was recruited to the Trump orbit purely for his ability to demagogue public opinion with his conspiracy theories. He continued to lie to the American people during his confirmation hearings in the Senate, when he said he would support vaccines if the data supported their safety. The data on vaccines is not in doubt; the only thing in doubt is whether Kennedy is more of a fool than the Republican senators, such as Bill Cassidy, who voted to confirm him.

When measles broke out in Texas and New Mexico in January 2025, Kennedy claimed that it was "not unusual" because "we have measles outbreaks every year." He claimed that patients were being hospitalized just to quarantine them, which was a lie. Instead of raising the alarm and urging nonvaccinated children to get the measles vaccine, Kennedy claimed that the choice should be personal. He said that vitamin A or cod liver oil might do the trick—a position most definitely not supported by the data. He even claimed that people couldn't die from infectious diseases, so any deaths must be from other causes. At least three people died during the outbreak, the first American deaths from measles since 2015. More than fifty people were hospitalized. By the end of the year, more than two thousand cases were reported, the most cases since the disease was declared eliminated twenty-five years ago. Not quite "not unusual."

The long-term impact on health is just as bad as the short-term impact on infectious diseases. When Kennedy and Trump pushed through their NIH cuts, they slashed funding for more than 74,000 patients in clinical trials. One in thirty trials was terminated, leaving patients exposed to more risk and setting medical science back for no good reason. Funding for the National Cancer Institute was cut by 31 percent in the first three months of Trump's first year back in power. The acting NIH director in particular asked that any grants involving mRNA be flagged for Kennedy's review. Vaccines built on mRNA science were key to ending the covid pandemic, so Kennedy and Trump bizarrely resent them. This is especially strange considering that Trump himself presided over Operation Warp Speed to quickly deploy vaccines during the pandemic.

In addition to their groundbreaking role in tackling covid, mRNA vaccines can be personalized to treat cancer. Clinical trials of mRNA vaccines have shown promising results in treating pancreatic cancer, which is normally untreatable, as well as melanoma. Personalized vaccines for melanoma could be available as early as 2028—if not for

Trump and Kennedy's vendetta against mRNA vaccines and medical research in general. An entire new set of weapons against cancer—vaccines that harness the power of our own immune system—is at risk because of their ignorance, their ideology, and their undemocratic power grab.

You can measure the health of a democracy by many standards: the fairness of its elections, the rule of law, the amount of corruption in government. But there are few measures as important as the health and well-being of its people. A healthy democracy should lead to a healthy population—not least because good health care, widely available, is something that voters will reward at the polls. Yet in Trump's America, thanks especially to the Supreme Court, the health of the American people is getting worse. If we cannot save the lives of Americans as well as other wealthy nations do, it's hard to explain why on earth we spend more on health care than they do.

* * *

The United States has achieved big, bold reforms to its health care system in living memory. And we're not talking about the patchwork of relatively minor reforms that make up Obamacare. Today it's political suicide to touch Medicare. Opinion polls show that more than 80 percent of Americans have a favorable view of Medicare, the government insurance program for people sixty-five and older. The number of Americans with a favorable view of Medicaid, the government program for low-income Americans, is not much different at 77 percent. Both government health care programs have clear majority support among every demographic and political group. Even among Trump voters, there's 62 percent support for Medicaid for those near the bottom of the economy. That's a far more socialist program than anything enacted by Obamacare.

Medicare and Medicaid were born in 1965 as part of what President Lyndon B. Johnson called his Great Society reforms. They were explicitly an attempt to build on Roosevelt's New Deal programs from a generation earlier. Johnson described his vision in a May 1964 speech at Ohio University: "It is a Society where no child will go unfed, and no youngster will go unschooled," he said. Johnson's so-called war on poverty included expanding Social Security to add health care for the first time. With supermajorities in Congress after his landslide election win in 1964, Johnson revolutionized American health care and politics. He signed it into law in Independence, Missouri, on July 30, 1964, with former president Harry Truman by his side at his presidential library. Truman had tried and failed to extend the New Deal to health care. Instead, he and his wife, Bess, became the first Americans to join Medicare two decades later.

"No longer will older Americans be denied the healing miracle of modern medicine," Johnson said when he created Medicare. "No longer will illness crush and destroy the savings that they have so carefully put away over a lifetime so that they might enjoy dignity in their later years. No longer will young families see their own incomes, and their own hopes, eaten away simply because they are carrying out their deep moral obligations to their parents, and to their uncles, and their aunts. And no longer will this Nation refuse the hand of justice to those who have given a lifetime of service and wisdom and labor to the progress of this progressive country."

Today, two in five Americans are covered by Medicare or Medicaid, representing around 145 million people. The two programs represent a huge commitment by the federal government. Together they cost more than $1.5 trillion a year, amounting to one-fifth of the entire federal budget. A slim majority of Americans believe that's not enough: 51 percent of Americans think the federal government should spend more on Medicare and Medicaid, while only 15 percent say it should spend less.

Over the years, various presidents and Congresses have added new provisions and benefits. Reagan added hospice benefits; Clinton expanded it to include health maintenance organizations (HMOs); George W. Bush extended it to prescription drugs. Much of Obamacare's expansion involved increasing the availability of Medicaid.

Still, Johnson's words about the crushing costs of health care ring true today. Before Obamacare, surveys showed that medical bills or bad health were the cause of 62 percent of bankruptcies in this country. In a 2018 follow-up study by researchers at Hunter College in New York, 59 percent of people who filed for bankruptcy said that medical expenses had contributed significantly to their financial collapse. In other words, Obamacare did not go far enough; it helped many Americans get medical insurance but did not save others from drowning in a sea of medical debt.

Even Obama himself acknowledges that Obamacare was not supposed to be the final word in health care reform. "I've always said that the Affordable Care Act is like a starter house: it was a big step forward, but still just a first step," he said on the fifteenth anniversary of signing it into law. "There's no question that we still have work to do to make sure that health care is a right and not a privilege in America."

According to the Consumer Financial Protection Bureau (before Trump dismantled it), around 100 million Americans owe more than $220 billion in medical debt. That includes around 3 million people who owe medical debt of more than $10,000 each.

A system that fails 100 million Americans—40 percent of all adults—is a system that is broken. A successful democracy would fix it—not with another patchwork of bandages that may or may not spark the outrage of the MAGA mob or big business. That's going to happen anyway. Obamacare tried to please everyone but has still ended up, all these years later, as one of the country's biggest bugbears.

The only solution that could help most Americans is Medicare for All: expanding the popular government system for the elderly to everyone. Instead of employers and employees paying premiums, taxes would pay for health care. Insurance companies could add supplemental care, as they do with Medicare today. But their vast profits would mostly disappear, as they should. In 2024, the seven largest American medical insurers reported a total $71.3 billion in profits, and their

CEOs were paid more than $146 million. It costs around $50 million to build a brand-new hospital in rural small-town America.

Medicare for All would be similar to Canada's public care system, which covers medically necessary services, which are free at the point of service, but not cosmetic procedures or private hospital rooms. Prescription drugs are generally not covered and need out-of-pocket payment or private insurance. The economic advantages are clear: Employers in Canada are more competitive because they aren't paying the health care costs that American employers have to pay, which can total tens of thousands of dollars per employee per year. Overall, health care costs are lower because the government (as a "single payer," hence "single-payer health care") can negotiate better prices and cut administrative costs on a large scale. According to a study published in *The Lancet*, Medicare for All would save more than $450 billion a year and save more than 68,000 lives.

This is an idea whose time has come. Much like the original Medicare, it may take decades to bring fundamental change to the American health care system. But when it arrives, its popularity will make it unstoppable. Medicare for All was first introduced as a bill in 2003, when the idea attracted only 39 percent support among Americans. Since 2016, when Bernie Sanders popularized the idea during his presidential campaign, the majority of Americans have said that they support a national health plan. That includes 77 percent of Democrats, 58 percent of independents, and 21 percent of Republicans, according to KFF polling.

Sanders believes that the political tide turned with the pandemic. "I think covid, where millions of people lost their jobs—and because their health care was attached to their jobs, they lost their health care—that made people think: Should health care simply be part of my job, as opposed to a basic right? That's number one," he told me. "And number two, what's happening right now with massive cuts to Medicaid and the ACA, people are also more conscious about how expensive health care in this country is—and how vulnerable they are if AI comes along and they lose their jobs. What are they going to do? As a nation we have got to make some very simple decisions. Do we agree with every other major country on Earth that health care is a human right? Should all of us have health care regardless of whether we're rich, we're poor, we're middle class, whether we're young or whether we're old? Overwhelmingly, people understand that this system is fundamentally broken, and we cannot just simply tinker around the edges."

The health care battles during Trump's budget cuts and the government shutdown were just the first round of a much bigger war. It won't be enough just to repair the damage Trump has caused, to patch up the holes he leaves behind. The day after Trump represents a once-in-a-generation opportunity to restore not just the health of our democracy but the health of Americans.

9

Breaking the News

Brendan Carr used to be just another pen pusher in Washington, DC, traveling the well-worn road between law firms and obscure government offices. It's generally a dull but lucrative career: nothing too flashy, nothing too famous, the kind of career that makes you courted by a handful of lobbyists who respect your regulatory power for the hot minute you have it. Carr was a law clerk for an appeals court judge, worked for a few years for a Washington law firm that specializes in business regulation, then joined the Federal Communications Commission as an attorney during the Obama years. He was an adviser to Ajit Pai, one of the FCC's Republican commissioners. Back in those pre-Trump days, it was traditional to keep agencies bipartisan. When Trump's first term began, Pai became FCC chair and Carr became general counsel.

Carr's first stint in a Trump FCC was nothing remarkable for a Republican-led agency. Pai advocated for less regulation and less uncertainty so businesses could be free to do their thing. He also introduced a new hotline number for suicide prevention. Carr soon became an FCC commissioner and focused on technical stuff such as the building of 5G towers. The toughest thing he did was to vote to roll back net neutrality, as the Trump FCC argued that government should not mess with the internet.

Back in the Obama years, Carr and Pai had been the first to push back when the FCC waded into anything that even hinted at politics. For instance, the Obama FCC proposed a study of how media organizations gather news, to assess whether they were meeting the "critical information needs" of the public. That would include areas such as health, politics, the environment, and the economy. It was just a study, mind you. But Carr's boss published an opinion piece in *The Wall Street Journal* blasting the study, and the FCC backed off. "The government has no place pressuring media organizations into covering certain stories," he wrote. Conservatives, led by the right-wing media machine, were outraged by the mere attempt to study media attitudes. What next? Carr's boss said that his goal was to "avoid having anyone in the government probing deeply into America's newsrooms." That was obviously another decade, in what looked like another country; the work of another Brendan Carr.

Halfway through the Biden years, Carr was introduced to the Heritage Foundation and its new work: preparing for the next Trump presidency based on a blueprint called Project 2025. Carr was an FCC commissioner, because the Democrats still believed in the bipartisan makeup of independent agencies. But he was paving the way to take the job of FCC chairman if Trump won—not least by courting the friendship of one Elon Musk. Carr welcomed Musk's purchase of Twitter and became a fanboy of his Starlink satellite internet business. He started complaining on social media that the FCC was harassing Musk. He said that the Democrats on the FCC were denying Starlink millions of dollars from a program to subsidize rural broadband. He even visited the SpaceX base in Texas and posed for photos with Musk. You see, government contracts mean a lot to the world's richest man. As it turns out, building a trillion-dollar fortune is not entirely about entrepreneurial innovation.

This is how fascism works: through the dull, plodding bureaucrats who cozy up to big business and then fall in love with a demagogue.

They are the ones who destroy the foundations of democracy because they know how to pull the levers of power. And they do so willingly, enthusiastically, because they are drunk on the power they know they have no legal right to wield.

Carr started to appear frequently on Fox News. He traveled to Mar-a-Lago during the presidential transition, and later wore a gold pin of Trump's face on his lapel. He even got to work before Trump was sworn into office, well before he was officially handed the leadership of the agency.

Just five weeks after the election, ABC News paid $15 million to settle a defamation lawsuit that Trump had filed because of a minor error on air. George Stephanopoulos had said, inaccurately, that Trump had been found liable in a civil lawsuit for raping the writer E. Jean Carroll. In fact, Trump had been found liable for sexually abusing and defaming Carroll. The jury in that case had ordered Trump to pay her damages of $5 million. Carroll sued a second time for defamation, based on Trump saying that he had never met her and her case was "a complete con job." A second jury ordered him to pay damages of $83 million.

To be clear, Carroll had accused Trump of rape. The jury had found in her favor but could not agree that the evidence fit the narrow legal definition of rape in New York State, involving Trump's penis. So they found him liable for sexual abuse. The judge in the case even said that Carroll had proved that Trump had raped her, "as many people commonly understand the word rape."

By any normal media standards, this would have been treated as an error worthy of a correction at most. A lawsuit worthy of a multimillion-dollar payout? Never. There's a reason why big media companies employ so many highly paid lawyers: to defend themselves against spurious lawsuits such as this. There are rock-solid protections for media companies in such situations. The First Amendment gives them broad free speech protection. Moreover, defamation is exceptionally hard to establish for a public figure, especially one whose reputation is already tarnished by, you know, paying off porn stars or bragging about grabbing women by their genitals. There's also the very high bar that requires plaintiffs to prove that the defendant acted with malice, demonstrating a knowing or reckless disregard for the truth. Simple mistakes are not enough to prove malice.

So why did ABC roll over and give Trump what it called a "charitable contribution" for his unbuilt presidential library, paying a sum that was three times what a jury had awarded to the victim of his sexual abuse? It even paid another $1 million to Trump's law firm. ABC News never explained its thinking, other than saying that it was pleased to have reached an agreement to dismiss the lawsuit. It signed the agreement on the same day a judge ordered Trump and Stephanopoulos to sit for depositions in the case.

How rare is this kind of media donation to a president? ABC News and its owner, the Walt Disney Company, have not made any public contributions to the Obama library. Disney's CEO, Bob Iger, made a donation through his personal foundation, but the media company— never mind its news division—has made no donation like its massive gift to Trump. You don't have to be a presidential historian to know how the right-wing echo chamber would have reacted if Disney had paid any money to Obama.

It isn't hard to understand the consequences. Disney is by far the largest of the old-media companies, with a market value around twice that of its nearest rival, Comcast, which owns NBC. By caving in to Trump's threats, it weakened every other media company before Trump even wielded power. And far from satiating Brendan Carr, the capitulation whetted his appetite, emboldening him to go back for more. Just one week after handing over $15 million as a sweetener, Iger received a letter from Carr about ABC's ongoing negotiations with local TV stations. "Americans no longer trust the national news media to report fully, accurately, and fairly," he wrote well before he was sworn in as the new chairman of the FCC. ". . . ABC's own conduct has certainly contributed to this erosion in public trust. For instance, ABC News recently agreed to pay $15 million to President Trump's future presidential foundation and museum and an additional $1 million in attorney fees to settle a defamation case."

Carr claimed that he was concerned about the complex negotiations going on between the network and its local affiliates about so-called retransmission fees, money that flows into stations from cable and satellite providers, which the networks like to take a cut of. But Carr wasn't really concerned about the financial health of local TV stations or their owners, which are often big media companies in their own right. What he seemingly wanted was leverage, another source of power over the biggest media players in the country. Forget about Carr's old objections to the Obama FCC studying how media organizations gather the news. The new Trumpy Carr was directly threatening the core business of the ABC television network—its relationship with its affiliate stations—by accusing its news coverage of bias.

It was just the prelude to what would happen less than a year after the election in the days after the assassination of the right-wing agitator Charlie Kirk. Kirk had made it his mission to troll and goad liberals all over the country. He believed that he was challenging woke orthodoxy while recruiting young Americans to his antiliberal crusade to turn back the clock to the 1950s. But he was also a passionate defender of free speech, not least because he argued that woke America was denying free speech on campuses, where he liked to work. "Hate speech does not exist legally in America," he posted on Twitter the year before he was murdered. "There's ugly speech. There's gross speech. There's evil speech. And ALL of it is protected by the First Amendment."

Except when the MAGA mob claims to be working in Kirk's name. At that point, there's no protected speech—especially not for late-night talk show comedians who frequently annoy Donald Trump by satirizing his buffoonery. Jimmy Kimmel, for instance, isn't the most edgy or political of those comedians: he's not Jon Stewart. But he works at ABC, which had already volunteered to be bullied, and he said something that could have been misconstrued: he suggested that right-wingers were playing politics with Kirk's murder, which they objectively were. "We hit some new lows over the weekend," he said on air, "with the MAGA gang desperately trying to characterize this kid who murdered Charlie Kirk as anything other than one of them and doing everything they can to score political points from it." Clumsy, yes. But otherwise pretty unremarkable—unlike the quip that followed, which mocked Trump for mourning like a child who'd lost his goldfish. Maybe the right-wingers were more offended by the satire than by the clumsy phrasing about the murderer.

It took the little fascist technocrat Brendan Carr to escalate that late-night snafu into a full-blown assault on the First Amendment and the biggest legacy media company in America. He appeared on *The Benny Show*, the podcast hosted by Benny Johnson, with his rhetorical knuckle-dusters and baseball bat at the ready. Johnson isn't just another right-wing media troll who passed through Breitbart, the Daily Caller, and Kirk's Turning Point USA; he was also fired by BuzzFeed News for plagiarism and pretended on social media that someone had set his DC home on fire "in an arson."

Carr told Johnson that Kimmel's comments were the "sickest conduct possible." He said that they were part of "a very concerted effort to try to lie to the American people" and explained that ABC needed the FCC's approval to operate its local stations. "They have a license granted by us at the FCC," he said, "and with that comes with it an obligation to operate in the public interest. And we can get into some ways that we've been trying to reinvigorate the public interest and some changes that we've seen. But frankly, when you see stuff like this, I mean, look, we can do this the easy way or the hard way. These companies can find ways to change conduct, to take action frankly on Kimmel, or there's going to be additional work for the FCC ahead."

Just hours later, Nexstar Media, the owner of many local stations across the country, pulled Kimmel's show off its schedule. Nexstar just happened to be in the middle of a $6.2 billion merger with its big rival Tegna, a deal that would require FCC approval to go ahead. It didn't take long after that for ABC to suspend Kimmel "indefinitely" in a decision made by CEO Bob Iger, who had already coughed up $16 million to mollify Trump.

It wasn't just the libs who were outraged by Carr's abuse of power. Ted Cruz, the Texas senator who is hardly the voice of political moderation, recognized the FCC chair's mob-style tactics. "I've got to say, that's right out of *Goodfellas*," he said on his own podcast. "That's right out of a mafioso coming into a bar going 'Nice bar you have here. It'd be a shame if something happened to it.'" Cruz's accent was criminally bad, but even he understood what Kirk had also identified: that free speech is actually free, and imposing government restrictions is a slippery slope—because a Democratic administration could use its FCC to do exactly what Carr was doing. "They will silence us," Cruz said. "They will use this power, and they will use it ruthlessly. And that is dangerous." It's nice to know that some people believe that the Democrats can be ruthless when in power.

In reality, the danger is not posed by some future administration; it's real and present, and it comes from the MAGA crowd. This goes far beyond the blatant, shameless hypocrisy of Brendan Carr, who pretended on Twitter in 2022 that he truly believed in the freedom of comedians to say what they wanted. "President Biden is right. Political satire is one of the oldest and most important forms of free speech," he wrote. "It challenges those in power while using humor to draw more people in to the discussion. That's why people in influential positions have always targeted it for censorship."

Even worse than the hypocrisy is the rapid descent into autocracy. Kimmel returned to his show a week later, after a huge public campaign to reinstate him. It took another week before Nexstar aired his show on its stations once again. But the damage was done. Disney employees received death threats. Attorney General Pam Bondi said that the Justice Department would "target you" if you posted what she called hate speech about Kirk's death. JD Vance brushed aside Carr's comments as a joke, but his boss endorsed them. "Keep up the GREAT work, Brendan," Trump posted on Truth Social.

This is how democracy dies and fascism takes hold: by creating a climate of fear in which people, no matter how rich and powerful, censor themselves. That fear is spread not just by the autocrat or his armed guards but by small-time middle managers who take it upon themselves to act like mob-style militia. People like Brendan Carr, a dull regulatory lawyer, who got high on his own supply as he sucked up to his leader.

* * *

One of the three party slogans in George Orwell's *1984* just about sums up the conservative media project that reached the apex of power in Trump's America: IGNORANCE IS STRENGTH. In Orwell's fictional future, the party maintains power not through knowledge but through lies. It's easier to control the masses that way. War is peace, freedom is slavery.

Orwell's warning about Communist dictatorship was only partially true. It wasn't just a Communist dictatorship that required an ignorant population to stay in power; there are also clear commercial interests in ignorance, especially when they overlap with the politics of the rich and powerful. You can build enormous profits and wield tremendous power by peddling lies that conform to your ideological purpose. In an era in which cable TV is in terminal decline, Fox News still reported annual income of almost $14 billion in 2024, with profits of $1.55 billion. It's a money machine that just happened to propel Donald Trump into power with a mantra that should be familiar: War is peace, and war makers should get the Nobel Peace Prize. Freedom is slavery, and talk of slavery is racist. Insurrection is patriotic, and the rule of law is a witch hunt. Ignorance is strength, and science is stupid.

Our long slide into stupidity and surreality is the result of decades of politics and profiteering. As television began to dominate the media in the postwar years, the FCC established the Fairness Doctrine. The idea was simple and public spirited: Since TV was broadcast on public airwaves, requiring government-issued licenses, TV stations needed to reflect the public's range of views on matters of public interest.

For two decades, the Fairness Doctrine was not in serious dispute. Then came the civil rights movement of the 1960s and a clear divide between the news coverage by national networks and the racist politics of some local stations. In 1969, a federal appeals court stripped the broadcast license from WLBT in Jackson, Mississippi, because it was aggressively pro-segregation and censored NBC's news coverage. That consensus ended in 1987, when the Republican-led FCC abolished the Fairness Doctrine in the name of free speech. Congress tried to protect it, but the legislation was vetoed by President Reagan.

What followed was a tidal wave of conservative talk radio that came to dominate the airwaves across the country. The year after the Fairness Doctrine died, Rush Limbaugh signed a national syndication contract to deliver his toxic mix of racist and sexist insults, combined with endless conspiracy theories and trolling of the libs. His show was free for local stations to carry, as long as they let his company sell ads. The model made everyone rich—and stupid—paving the way for people such as Alex Jones, who claimed that the 2012 Sandy Hook massacre was a hoax. When Limbaugh died in 2021, he was earning an annual salary of $85 million.

The Limbaugh-led radio revolution was mirrored on television thanks to the singular talents of Roger Ailes. Ailes was a twenty-eight-year-old TV producer when he joined the Nixon campaign with a group of admen, public relations advisers, and TV executives. They were the first to package a president for the era of TV advertising that we all know so well.

Nixon had bombed in his first TV debate against the youthful John F. Kennedy in 1960. In his second run for the presidency, in 1968, he would not make the same mistake again. Ailes had first met Nixon in 1967 when he'd been a guest on the daytime talk show that Ailes was producing. "It's a shame a man has to use gimmicks like this to get elected," Nixon told Ailes, according to the bestselling book about that campaign, *The Selling of the President 1968*. "Television is not a gimmick," Ailes replied. Nixon liked that thinking and ordered his staff to hire Ailes.

Ailes worked alongside Harry Treleaven, who understood that issues bored voters; what mattered was image. Treleaven had learned all he needed to know from his first campaign, the long-shot congressional race of the son of a Connecticut senator named George H. W. Bush. No Republican had ever won his Texas district, and Bush started 8 points behind. He eventually won by 16 points, after spending 80 percent of his budget on advertising. "Political candidates are celebrities," Treleaven wrote.

Together they smoothed over Nixon's rough edges, managed his TV appearances carefully, and minimized his dislikable image and character. Nixon squeaked by with a narrow victory in the 1968 campaign, in no small part thanks to the third-party campaign by former Alabama Governor George Wallace, who ran as a brazenly pro-segregation candidate. Ailes worked with the Nixon White House to push more pro-Nixon news on the national TV networks, instead of focusing on newspapers. TV, he argued, was far more important than print or radio. "The reason: People are lazy," he wrote in a memo. "With television you just sit—watch—listen. The thinking is done for you."

After Nixon was driven from the presidency, Ailes spent a short time working on an ill-fated attempt in the mid-1970s to launch a syndicated TV news service that was supposed to be a conservative alternative to the major networks. Television News Inc. was funded by Joseph Coors, the brewing magnate who helped set up the Heritage Foundation. The business was a failure, but the idea never died. Ailes spent the 1980s electing Ronald Reagan and then George H. W. Bush before returning to TV at NBC, then owned by General Electric. He created *America's Talking*, a cable talk show channel whose hosts included Steve Doocy (later to work on Fox News), Chris Matthews (later to work on MSNBC), and E. Jean Carroll (later to sue Donald Trump). Ailes wanted NBC to launch a conservative channel, but NBC wanted to stay in its traditional, politically neutral zone. The channel turned into MSNBC in 1996 as a cheap version of CNN, a decade before it became a progressive outlet.

Ailes took his idea for a conservative channel to News Corporation and its conservative chairman, Rupert Murdoch. Fox News was launched in 1996 with a novel business model: Instead of being paid by cable providers, Fox paid the providers to take its channel. That was even more attractive than Rush Limbaugh's deal with radio stations across the country. It was Ailes who coined the network's initial and long-running slogan, "Fair and balanced"—not because the channel was objectively fair and balanced but as a wink and a nod to its conservative audience about liberal bias. Everything else was unfair and unbalanced, so Fox News was just righting the ship.

Donald Trump owes his political rise and his power to two media creations. One is NBC's reality show *The Apprentice*, which portrayed him as a supremely successful and skilled business leader despite all the evidence—in his career and on-screen—pointing in the opposite direction. The second was the audience convened and catalyzed by Fox News in the two decades before Trump was first elected.

That audience was fed a daily diet that reflected Roger Ailes's twisted personality and ideological mission. Ailes liked to carry a gun with him, hid behind his personal security team, and constantly feared that some group or other was out to attack him. If you watched Fox News, you would have thought the same. After the 9/11 attacks, the Muslim terrorists were out to get you. During the Obama years, the socialists and foreigners were out to get you. Sometimes it was the New Black Panther Party; sometimes it was the migrant caravan. In any case, the average Fox News viewer—overwhelmingly white and over fifty years old—needed to know that their lives were at risk from all sorts of outside threats and the amorphous blob they call "the mainstream."

What they mean by "the mainstream" is liberal America, and "the mainstream media" is their smear on traditional outlets such as NBC and *The New York Times*. In reality, Fox News, whether on cable or broadcast, dominates all TV news coverage today. It beats not just

CNN and MSNBC but ABC, CBS, and NBC. It is, in fact, the mainstream news of the Trump era. Fox News Radio even dominates conservative talk radio today.

Ailes succeeded because he created enormous wealth for News Corporation and Rupert Murdoch, who generally supported his ideological mission. His frequent excesses could be excused in the name of profit and politics. His partisan purpose was perfectly suited to the ultracompetitive landscape of cable TV. In a sea of hundreds of channels, you needed to stand out. Broadcasting partisan "news" was a great way to separate yourself from the crowd and build deep personal loyalty among viewers. What brought him down was not his politics but his attitude and behavior toward women, especially his sexual harassment of his own employees.

Money, politics, and misogyny. If that sounds like Donald Trump, that's because it is. It may not have been planned in quite this way, at least not for the benefit of someone quite as crazy. But Fox News built MAGA America for Trump to take power.

* * *

Under Trump's second coming, the Foxification of the media has accelerated. Media companies are not just acquiescing to Trump's coercion; they are actively turning themselves into pale imitations of a Roger Ailes creation.

The leader of the pack is Skydance Media, which in August 2025 bought Paramount in an $8 billion deal that includes the movie studios, the CBS broadcast network, and Paramount's cable channels such as Comedy Central and Nickelodeon. The deal sailed through the FCC approval process because Brendan Carr had already shaken down his targets. In particular, he was ready to take his metaphorical baseball bat to CBS News because of a discrepancy between two edits of a *60 Minutes* interview with Kamala Harris in the final weeks of the 2024 presidential campaign. The difference between the two interviews was microscopic. But it was all Trump needed to claim that he'd been the victim of a great media conspiracy. Even less than the ABC News error, the CBS News edit was barely worthy of a clarification, never mind a correction. The slim pickings didn't deter Trump from filing a $20 billion lawsuit—that's billion with a *b*—against CBS and Paramount in October 2024. Astonishingly, the media company agreed to enter into mediation about Trump's fantastical lawsuit, whereas in normal times it would have laughed its way to a legal equivalent of flipping the bird. Along the way, it forced out the executive producer of *60 Minutes*, Bill Owens, who resigned from his position in April 2025 rather than cave to political or commercial extortion. And in July 2025, it agreed to a nonsensical $16 million settlement, which just happened to be the same number ABC had paid the nonexistent Trump presidential library six months earlier.

The bed-wetting did not stop there. The same month Paramount dumped a pile of cash into Trump's lap, it canceled *The Late Show with Stephen Colbert*, which had been the most pointedly anti-Trump of all the late-night talk shows. That was just three days after its host, Stephen Colbert, called the $16 million deal "a big fat bribe." CBS claimed that the show had been canceled for financial reasons.

Within weeks, Brendan Carr waved the deal through. Why so soon? Was it the $16 million big fat bribe? The cancellation of Colbert and the caving at *60 Minutes*? Was it the promise of an ombudsman to root out supposed bias at CBS News? Or possibly Trump's claim that CBS News would give him $26 million of free airtime? All the above—and so much more. Because Skydance is not your ordinary media company; it's more like another Fox News, politically aligned with Trump and more than ready to intervene on behalf of their shared political mission. Skydance is owned and run by David Ellison, a son of the tech titan Larry Ellison, who is worth around $400 billion. Larry Ellison has been a top conservative donor for at least a decade and even took part in a call to challenge the 2020 election results. One of David Ellison's first moves as owner of Paramount was to appoint Bari Weiss, a conservative opinion columnist who loves to hate liberals, as editor in chief of CBS News. That was after he paid her an eye-popping $150 million to buy her Substack newsletter.

Whatever Ellison may be, he is not a savvy businessman if he pays those kinds of prices for a newsletter that might scrape together $20 million in annual revenue. And whatever Weiss may be, she is not an editor in chief of a network news organization. Together, they are ideological soulmates, trying to Foxify a legacy media company.

The phenomenon is not exactly subtle. Trump is reshaping the media landscape to maintain and extend his grip on power. The Ellisons are merely grabbing their opportunity in that Trump-shaped hole in our democracy. "Larry Ellison is great, and his son David is great. They're friends of mine. They're big supporters of mine," Trump told reporters on Air Force One. "They will make the right decisions. They're going to revitalize CBS. Hopefully, they'll bring it back to its former glory." He was musing about changes at CBS just as the Ellisons were putting together a bid to buy Warner Bros. Discovery in a $60 billion deal that would give them control not just of another movie studio but also of cable channels including HBO and CNN.

With legacy news organizations in their pocket, the Ellisons could do anything Trump wants. Sure enough, White House officials made it clear that they wanted to see the Ellisons take over Warner Bros. Discovery. They even talked about the programming changes they wanted to see at CNN. It turns out they aren't all that interested in the next season of *The White Lotus* on HBO.

For other media giants, that might be galling, but it's just the way the game is played in an autocracy. Comcast, the owner of NBC, tried joining the corporate fawning and bribery. It donated millions of dollars to Trump's new ballroom at the White House, even though there was no transparency in the donations, the demolition, or the construction—not a good look for a communications company but a great look for a corporate giant looking to curry favor with an autocratic leader. It was just never going to be enough to appease someone who hates Comcast's progressive MSNBC cable channel, even if it was renamed and spun out of the company as MS NOW.

If you're going to Foxify yourself, you need to switch your politics. You need to neuter your criticism. You need to stop being the arbiter of truth and embrace the notion that ignorance is strength.

That was what Jeff Bezos did at *The Washington Post*, under the guise of broadening the appeal of his newspaper. First, he intervened personally to spike his newspaper's endorsement of Kamala Harris before the 2024 election. That was after a decade of ownership during which time he had intervened precisely zero times in the paper's coverage. "Presidential endorsements do nothing to tip the scales of an election," he wrote. ". . . What presidential endorsements actually do is create a perception of bias. A perception of non-independence. Ending them is a principled decision, and it's the right one." It was so right that three members of his editorial board quit and thousands of readers canceled their subscriptions. But who cares about those people when you're making a "principled decision," right?

What matters is the perception of bias—such as the perception of bias that might arise when executives from Blue Origin met with one Donald Trump soon after the Harris endorsement was killed. Blue Origin is the space travel company that Bezos loves more than any other part of his empire. He said he'd had no advance knowledge of the meeting, so that's all fine and dandy when you're worried about the perception of bias.

Bezos is so committed to avoiding a perception of bias, so avidly independent, that he scrapped the entire opinion section just a month after Trump's inauguration. Instead of printing a range of political opinions, the new, nonbiased *Post* would now focus on "personal liberties and free markets"—in other words, exactly what the right-wing opinion pages of *The Wall Street Journal* have done for decades. This highly independent decision led to the resignation of the Post's well-respected opinion editor, David Shipley, who had previously led the free market–loving opinion section of Bloomberg. The *Post* insisted that its new right-wing opinion pages were not intended to support one political party or another. But they proceeded to hire a new opinion editor, Adam O'Neal, who worked previously as an editorial page writer at the explicitly and consistently right-wing *Wall Street Journal.*

You'll be astonished to hear that O'Neal gave his first interview in his new job to the Fox News website, where he explained that his mission was to alienate his current audience in the hope of finding a new one. "Our readers are overwhelmingly liberal, right? And they're all overwhelmingly located in blue states," he said, before conceding that they would probably be offended by his new opinion pages. ". . . Maybe that's true. But looking forward as I rebuild, I really just see it as an opportunity to expand our reach. And frankly, a lot of people don't trust The Post. And they don't trust the mainstream media more broadly."

Jeff Bezos may be clunky at politics, but he is above all a savvy businessman. Why would someone who built himself one of the biggest fortunes in the world decide to alienate his own customers? How does the Foxification of *The Washington Post* make any business sense? The answer lies not in the business model of a dying newspaper but in the billions of dollars of federal government contracts held by Amazon Web Services (AWS). In August 2025, just six months after Foxifiying the *Post*, AWS agreed to a massive deal to modernize the tech infrastructure across the federal government, promising $1 billion in savings. Its national security contracts alone are worth almost $20 billion.

* * *

Democracies don't just fall off a cliff; they get pushed. First an autocrat wins an election and seizes full power. The legislature becomes a puppet. The courts lose their independence. Businesses prostrate themselves to make money. The only surviving check and balance is the media. So the media's independence is hacked back through extorting its corporate owners with threats, nuisance lawsuits, and government "oversight." The free press dies not with a bang but with a bunch of wimps. That's the story of Vladimir Putin's Russia, Viktor Orbán's Hungary, and Recep Tayyip Erdoğan's Turkey. Their countries used to enjoy a vibrant choice of media. Now the surviving independent voices are few and far between—if not in real danger.

You soon end up with a wannabe dictator who pulls the kind of stunts that we Americans used to laugh at. He unilaterally changes the names of places from Tsaritsyn to Stalingrad or from the Gulf of Mexico to the Gulf of America. If you don't agree to the name change, you're banished, as the Associated Press discovered. He appoints TV stars to run government departments as propaganda arms, such as Dmitry Kiselyov, who went seamlessly from being a TV presenter to running Russian state media. Or Pete Hegseth, who went seamlessly from cohosting a weekend show on Fox News to running the biggest department in the federal government, which used to be called the Department of Defense. That was until the wannabe dictator changed its name—at a cost of up to $2 billion—to the Department of War. From there the former TV host promptly banished all media that refused to have their stories approved by the government.

The wannabe dictator even orders up movies that make him feel good or just make him rich. Trump pushed Paramount to produce the embarrassingly poor *Rush Hour 4* movie that nobody else wanted to support, because he liked the aging franchise—and because he liked its director Brett Ratner, who had been accused by several women of sexual harassment. Ratner's other new project just happens to be a documentary about First Lady Melania Trump. That documentary somehow raised a staggering $40 million payout from a very well-connected media and tech giant called Amazon. Thanks, Jeff!

It is easier to demolish the news business than it is to build it. Rebuilding a free press will take time, not least because it cannot be controlled by democratically minded officials. That's the point of the media, after all. A post-Trump government can certainly rebuild the Voice of America and its associated outlets, but those are explicitly state-owned media channels with the goal of challenging dictatorships around the world. Reshaping the media at home will be more complicated because of the digital revolution, which continues to transform what Americans consume and how they consume it.

Still, there are steps that a new president and Congress can take, such as strictly limiting the FCC's powers, to stop another Brendan Carr from bullying and meddling with the legacy media; such as not just restoring funding for PBS television and NPR stations but going further by creating an independent media fund that could revive small-town newspapers that have been destroyed by the shift to online advertising; such as repealing Section 230 of the Communications Decency Act of 1996, which protects online giants from liability for what their creators can post and publish. If social media companies were treated like newspaper publishers or TV networks, they would find a way to stop the disinformation that is so toxic to any democracy. There would be no space for Alex Jones to defame the grieving families of Sandy Hook or for Russian and North Korean propaganda factories to smear and intimidate elected US officials.

The big tech companies certainly have the resources to do so. Alphabet, the parent company of Google and YouTube, reported profits of more than $100 billion in 2024. Meta, the parent company of Facebook and Instagram, reported profits of more than $60 billion in the same year. For context, each one of those companies dwarfs the entire American newspaper industry at its peak. In the early 2000s, the total revenue of every newspaper combined across the country was around $49 billion. That's less than the profits of Meta in 2024.

On the face of it, there are far more important priorities than the media on the day after Trump leaves office: the economy, health care, and the Supreme Court, to name a few. However, you cannot underestimate the importance of the free press in a free country. The second president of our republic, John Adams, wrote into the Massachusetts Constitution, "The liberty of the press is essential to the security of freedom in a state: it ought not, therefore, to be restrained in this commonwealth."

Why did the founding fathers believe that freedom of the press was so important? Because a democracy relies on its informed citizens. "Liberty cannot be preserved without a general knowledge among the people, who have a right, from the frame of their nature, to knowledge," Adams wrote in September 1765.

Two hundred and fifty years later, those words are still true. Ignorance is not strength; it weakens us as citizens, and it strengthens wannabe dictators. The fight for media independence is not a fight for the freedom of TV producers or movie studios; it's a fight for our own freedom.

10

Greenhouse Gas

They had such a good thing going, Donald Trump and Elon Musk. In the early weeks of Trump's second term, Musk posted that he loved Trump "as much as a straight man can love another man." They had campaigned together and spent the transition period together at Mar-a-Lago. Trump called Musk a supergenius. Musk said he wasn't just MAGA, he was "dark MAGA." Trump gave Musk free rein to slash government departments and budgets, no matter how much his own cabinet secretaries disagreed. That's what $290 million of campaign donations will buy you.

Summer loving happened so fast. After four months of chaos and vandalism, Musk stepped down from his pedestal of unrivaled power, his ears ringing with lavish praise from Trump. "He had to go through the slings and arrows, which is a shame because he's an incredible patriot," Trump said as he handed Musk a large golden key with his signature on it. It was a gift reserved only for "very special people," he said of the tchotchke. It almost made up for the way Musk had destroyed the Tesla brand by serving as Trump's axman.

Within months, the bromance died in a flurry of angry tweets and angrier posts on Truth Social. Musk dared to call bullshit on the "big beautiful bill" of tax cuts. "This massive, outrageous, pork-filled Congressional spending bill is a disgusting abomination," Musk posted on Twitter on June 3, 2025. In an Oval Office meeting on June 6, Trump said that he was "very disappointed because Elon knew the inner workings of this bill better than almost anybody sitting here." He threatened to end Musk's government contracts. Musk said that Trump would have lost the election without his money. For good measure, as he slammed the door shut, he said that Trump was all over the Epstein files, which is "the real reason they have not been made public." To think that Trump had bought a red Tesla Model S just a few weeks earlier, on the South Lawn of the White House, of all places.

Even more important than the end of the bromance was the crux of the beef between them: the end of the electric vehicle tax credit. "Elon is upset because we took the EV mandate, and you know, which was a lot of money for electric vehicles. . . . they want us to pay billions of dollars in subsidy," Trump said in the Oval Office on June 5, sitting beside the chancellor of Germany, who looked like he was hoping the earth would open up and swallow him whole. In response, Musk pretended not to care about the tax credits. "Whatever," he posted. That's how it is when a relationship breaks down. It's a tale as old as time; both sides claim victory and feign indifference.

Amid their many lies, both men were telling some degree of truth. Musk's Tesla business did indeed benefit from the $7,500-per-car subsidy. And Trump didn't really care about the cost of the subsidies. What he actually opposed was any part of the green economy, especially the parts boosted by Joe Biden's Inflation Reduction Act. In reality, the tax credits had been in place since the end of the Bush years. They had been expanded at the start of the Obama years and extended into Trump's first term without any problem. Biden had expanded them again when he lifted the cap on manufacturers' claiming the tax credits, which had stood at 200,000 vehicles per manufacturer.

The tax credits had been hugely successful. A study by Stanford

University economists found that for every dollar of the tax credits, the US economy had reaped $1.87 of benefits, not least because the Inflation Reduction Act required the electric vehicles to be assembled in North America, with their main components sourced from the United States or its allies. The subsidies weren't just helping to drive the transition from fossil fuels to a clean-energy economy; they were also tilting the market in ways that would hurt our biggest economic rival and Trump's personal bogeyman, China. Along the way, they were also boosting the US auto manufacturing industry, which is supposedly one of Trump's main goals. But the tax credits were a Biden thing, and all Biden things are stupid, according to the biggest-brained president in living memory—even if the Biden thing involves beating Trump's biggest international rival.

When Biden's team explained its green economic strategy, they did not leave the job to their economic team. They chose instead to explain the bigger national mission in a speech by the national security advisor, Jake Sullivan—because the green economy is part of the geopolitical chess game, not just a matter of global survival (which *should* be enough, but alas). "We are leveraging the Inflation Reduction Act to build a clean-energy manufacturing ecosystem rooted in supply chains here in North America, and extending to Europe, Japan, and elsewhere," Sullivan said. The need for that ecosystem included sourcing supply chains for critical minerals and batteries from our allies, rather than relying on China, a rival, for those precious resources. The United States produces only 4 percent of the lithium it needs, 13 percent of the cobalt, and none of the nickel and graphite. "Clean-energy supply chains are at risk of being weaponized in the same way as oil in the 1970s, or natural gas in Europe in 2022," he explained.

Trump found out the hard way that the Biden team—along with every other international economist and industry specialist—was correct: Reliance on China for rare-earth metals is a fundamentally weak position, especially when you're trying to squeeze China on global trade with punitive tariffs. All it took was for the Chinese to restrict rare-earth exports to push Trump into a trade truce. When Trump caved in to Chinese pressure, some American factories were weeks away from stopping production without more shipments of Chinese rare-earth metals and magnets, according to industry analysts.

So why was Trump so determined to self-destruct on the clean-energy economy? Why would he want to hurt American manufacturers and hand more power to China?

While no one wants to take on the unenviable task of trying to figure out what passes for thinking inside Trump's skull, there are some clues. Back in 2006, a full decade before his surprise victory over Hillary Clinton, Trump bought a golf course in Aberdeenshire, Scotland. A few years later, the Scottish government wanted to install eleven wind turbines alongside his golf course. Trump objected, appearing before the Scottish Parliament to complain about the damage they would cause to tourism. The Scottish government went ahead anyway, and Trump continued to call them "windmills," which he said were "some of the ugliest you've ever seen." He was still moaning about them when he flew to Scotland thirteen years later, in the summer of his first year back in power, saying that the United Kingdom should "get rid of the windmills and bring back the oil."

The Aberdeen Bay Wind Farm generates enough electricity to supply up to eighty thousand homes. It was designed to test the new technology that could help Scotland transition to clean, sustainable energy. Since they were built, Scotland has more than doubled the number of installed wind turbines, with plans to generate enough power for 45 million homes by 2040. Trump was talking about bringing back North Sea oil in Scotland, but he's already too late. Oil output near Scotland peaked in 1999.

Standing next to the British prime minister at his golf course, Trump complained that the wind farms were killing birds. It was a touching moment of concern for wildlife by a president who is more than happy to open up the entire coastal plain of the pristine Arctic National Wildlife Refuge to oil and gas drilling. As conservation groups have made clear, drilling in the Arctic refuge would destroy one of the most ecologically important corners of the planet, which is vital for polar bears, migratory birds, and the porcupine caribou. There are, however, no Trump golf courses nearby. So the Scottish birds are much, much more important.

If only the birds had known about the dangers of the wind turbines. A two-year study by the British Trust for Ornithology attached cameras to the wind towers to detect and track birds passing by. It was part of a worldwide study to understand how birds respond to wind farms. The researchers did not record a single bird strike.

"Wind is a disaster," Trump said. ". . . Wind is the most expensive form of energy, and it destroys the beauty of your fields and your plains and your waterways. . . . When we go to Aberdeen, you'll see some of the ugliest windmills you've ever seen. They're the height of a fifty-story building, and you can take a thousand times more energy out of a hole in the ground this big. This big. It's called oil and gas, and you have it there, the North Sea. This big that nobody would even see. You can take a thousand times more power because the wind is intermittent. It doesn't work. It's extremely expensive. All the windmills are made in China." He ranted about how the wind turbines rust at sea. He also explained how the blades don't rust and can't be disposed of safely. And he talked about why he had killed wind power in the United States.

"I restricted windmills in the United States because they also kill all your birds," he said. "You know, they wipe out—you know, it's interesting. If you shoot a bald eagle in the United States, they put you in jail for five years. And yet windmills knock out hundreds of them. They don't do anything. You explain that. So it's a very expensive energy. It's a very ugly energy. And we won't allow it in the United States."

Keir Starmer, the British prime minister, politely responded that wind energy was here to stay as part of a mix of renewable energy sources.

For the record, the cost of wind and solar energy is cheaper than fossil fuels, according to analysts at Lazard. For the record, wind turbines don't kill all the birds. And for the record, windmills turn grain into flour. Wind turbines turn wind into power.

* * *

This is not a drill. Trump's half-baked thinking about clean energy is a full-blown disaster for our country and our planet. It's as self-destructive as it is delusional. In a functional democracy, there would be no room for this nonsense. The safety and well-being of our fellow Americans, as well as our fellow humans, depend on our leaders' protecting us from the extreme weather and rising sea levels that the climate crisis has already triggered. Our economic growth, including the creation of thousands of new jobs, relies on smart policies that can transition us to clean energy.

Instead, we have surrendered unchecked power to a whimsical autocrat who sees the climate crisis as a great way to demagogue his voters and distract them from reality. It is, after all, much easier to convince the MAGA mob that the libs want to snatch away their gas-guzzling pickup truck than it is to explain clean-vehicle tax credits. Conspiracies beat the climate crisis drum seven days a week and twice on Sunday.

How do you know that Trump is lying? It's not just because he's moving his lips. The real tell is when he accuses everyone else of lying. Call it projection, distraction, or whataboutism, Trump is a shameless showman when it comes to lying about the climate crisis. He even did so in front of the UN General Assembly in September 2025. First, naturally, he talked about windmills in Scotland before warming up to his theme of climate predictions that had not panned out. "It used to be global cooling," he said. "If you look back years ago in the 1920s and the 1930s, they said, 'Global cooling will kill the world. We have to do something.' Then they said, 'Global warming will kill the world.' But then it started getting cooler. So now they could just call it climate change because that way they can't miss. Climate change because if it goes higher or lower, whatever the hell happens, it's climate change.

"It's the greatest con job ever perpetrated on the world, in my opinion," said the man who knows a thing or two about great con jobs. ". . . All of these predictions made by the United Nations and many others, often for bad reasons, were wrong. They were made by stupid people that have cost their countries fortunes and given those same countries no chance for success. If you don't get away from this green scam, your country is going to fail."

Here's what really happened: The ten years from 2015 to 2024 were the ten warmest years on record, and 2024 was the warmest year ever. That's according to the World Meteorological Organization, the UN agency tasked with serving as the world's authority on climate. In fact, 2024 was so warm that it was the first calendar year more than 1.5 degrees Celsius above the preindustrial average. Climate scientists had set the 1.5-degree mark as the tipping point for the most severe and irreversible impacts of climate change. That was the mark included in the Paris Agreement in 2015, when two hundred countries, including the United States, agreed to take steps to limit greenhouse gas emissions to stop the worst effects of a warming planet. Once the planet warms above the plus-1.5-degree mark, we risk the breakdown of ocean circulation systems, the rapid thawing of permafrost, and the collapse of ice sheets and coral reefs.

But that's just the world's authority on climate science. On the other side, we have Donald Trump, who told the UN General Assembly, "I'm really good at predicting things. They actually said during the campaign, they had a hat, the best-selling hat: 'Trump was right about everything.' And I don't say that in a braggadocious way, but it's true. I've been right about everything. And I'm telling you that if you don't get away from the green energy scam, your country is going to fail."

Science and data pose a fundamental challenge to a guy whose claim to expert status is a baseball hat that says he's right about everything. It's a challenge to his authority and of course his ego, not least because it opens the door to alternative policies and decisions—you know, the kind of stuff that healthy democracies do, with policy debates and political opposition.

Trump's plan is not just to make bad speeches that frankly embarrass the United States on the world stage; it's to erase data and science. Since 1980, the National Oceanic and Atmospheric Administration has kept a database tracking every extreme weather event that caused more than $1 billion of damage. Over that time, it has recorded more than four hundred events that cost the country more than $2.9 trillion and almost seventeen thousand lives. That data has been important not just for scientists but also for insurers and policymakers. It was shut down in May of Trump's first year back in power, and the MAGA mob celebrated. Brian Babin, a Texas Republican congressman who chairs the House Science, Space, and Technology Committee, claimed that the NOAA database was "riddled with scientific and methodological flaws" and was pushing "political narratives dressed up as science." Those "political narratives" were the ones linking climate change to extreme weather events.

The elimination of the NOAA database was just one part of Trump's assault on climate science. In his first week back in power, he fired all the scientific advisers to the Environmental Protection Agency (EPA), including those advising on clean-air science. He followed up by firing EPA staff working on climate change and freezing $20 billion in EPA funds for greenhouse gas reduction. He canceled funding for the U.S. Global Change Research Program, which issues a comprehensive report every four years, the National Climate Assessment, on how climate change is affecting every region in the country. His administration set about scrubbing any mention of climate science from federal websites, including the Department of Agriculture, the EPA, the Federal Emergency Management Agency (FEMA), and the Department of Energy.

In July 2025, the whiz kids at the Department of Energy published a report claiming that warming caused by carbon dioxide emissions "appears to be less damaging economically than commonly believed, and that aggressive mitigation strategies could be more harmful than beneficial." Trump's energy experts even said that "U.S. policy actions are expected to have undetectably small direct impacts on the global climate and any effects will emerge only with long delays."

It's amazing how the Trumpy simulation of science has proved the baseball hat correct.

Trump's climate denial extends beyond the science and data. On his first day back in power, he froze unspent funds from the Inflation Reduction Act and withdrew from the Paris Agreement for the second time. He ended the American Climate Corps, which was training young Americans for jobs in clean energy and conservation. He expanded offshore drilling and revoked approval for those much loathed offshore wind farms. Countless regulations and rules to limit the effects of climate change and promote green economy jobs have been suspended or rescinded.

It's only when we are swimming in a warm sea of ignorance that a president can tell the world, with a straight face, that carbon emissions are meaningless because Barack Obama flew on Air Force One. No, seriously, that was what Trump told the United Nations General Assembly: "The carbon footprint is a hoax made up by people with evil intentions and they're heading down a path of total destruction. The carbon footprint, it was a big, big thing. A few years ago, I remember hearing about the carbon footprint and then President Obama would get into Air Force One, a massive Boeing 747, and not a new one, an old one with old engines that spew everything into the atmosphere. He talked about the carbon footprint. 'We must do . . .' Then he'd get in and he'd fly from Washington to Hawaii to play a round of golf, and then he'd get back onto that big, beautiful plane and he'd fly back and he'd talk about, again, global warming and the carbon footprint. It's a con job at extreme costs and expense."

After sarcastically congratulating Europe for lowering carbon emissions, he lamented that there were still a few people back home who believed in climate science. "In the United States, we have still radicalized environmentalists, and they want the factories to stop," he said. "Everything should stop. No more cows. We don't want cows anymore. I guess they want to kill all the cows. They want to do things that are just unbelievable."

It is indeed unbelievable. You can literally not believe any of the words Trump says about climate change. Not about the killing of the cows. Not about the pointlessness of reducing carbon emissions. Not even about Obama flying to Hawaii just to play a round of golf. On his own MAGA terms, he is making no sense. The most unbelievable part of his absurd position on the climate crisis is the business advantage he's handing to his mortal enemies in China. It's almost as though he sees more value in peddling conspiracies to his MAGA voters than he does in helping American businesses beat the competition around the world.

Dominating energy is a proven path to global power. Just ask the Saudis and the other Gulf states. In the new-energy economy, there is one country that's already dominant: China. For the last twenty years, China has been responsible for the largest fossil fuel emissions in the world. But that changed in 2024, when they declined—albeit slightly—for the first time. As Trump was declaring climate change to be some twisted hoax, China promised to cut its greenhouse gas emissions by up to 10 percent over the next ten years. How could it shift course like that? Because it's investing in clean energy far more than any other country. In 2024, it built twice the wind and solar capacity of the rest of the world combined. All the top wind turbine and solar panel producers are Chinese, and the country has stormed into a commanding lead in electric vehicle manufacturing, too. Renewable energy sources now account for more than half of all power generation in China.

So Trump and the Republicans who enable him are failing both their country and the world. It's not just a matter of science; they're also failing in business and national security. They are even failing his own MAGA voters. The U.S. Climate Vulnerability Index is a project by Texas A&M University to score each region of the country on the basis of local stability in terms of environmental, social, economic, and infrastructure factors. It has found that the parts of the country most vulnerable to extreme weather conditions are almost entirely in the Republican strongholds of the Deep South and Appalachia.

You don't need to be a university researcher to see what's going on. In July 2025, at least 135 people died in destructive floods along the Guadalupe River in central Texas. The river rose twenty-six feet in just forty-five minutes as more than six inches of rain fell in three hours. The death toll included twenty-seven girls and counselors at Camp Mystic, a Christian summer camp, built on an area that FEMA estimated had a 1 percent chance of severe flooding. That hundred-year chance of a flood happened just two months before Trump trashed climate change at the United Nations. The risk of catastrophic flooding was supposed to be so low that the county was refused funding for a flood warning system.

Instead of dealing with the unimaginable tragedies of the floods, Texas Governor Greg Abbott focused his attention on Trump's needs for more gerrymandering in his state. He called a special session of the legislature just five days after the worst of the floods, as more than 160 people were still missing.

That was less than a year after the floods in North Carolina in which more than a hundred people died in catastrophic floods in western Appalachia. The floods were triggered by historic rainfall caused by Hurricane Helene, after it swept inland from the Florida coast. It was the most expensive natural disaster in the state's history. In Asheville, almost ten inches of rain fell in just two days.

FEMA said that less than 1 percent of homes in the affected counties in North Carolina had flood insurance. That's because Congress prevents FEMA from using climate change forecasts to create its own flood maps. It's restricted to making projections based on past floods, leaving homeowners at risk and underinsured. Local officials are happy to play along with the smaller flood maps because they require builders to follow tougher construction guidelines, and homeowners need to purchase costly insurance. In fact, the flood maps covering Asheville were last updated fourteen years before the deadly catastrophe. North Carolina was still rebuilding roads and bridges damaged by the floods as Republicans began their extreme gerrymandering in *that* state a year later.

Climate denial is costly and by no means limited to Donald Trump. It's the result of a democracy that no longer prioritizes the safety, security, and prosperity of its citizens. For the MAGA mob, climate denial is a perfect conspiracy to scare their own voters. It plays on their fears of change, their confusion about science, and the very human preference for kicking the can down the road. *They* are conning you. *They* are coming after your way of life. *They* don't understand you. Until a once-in-a-century flood comes raging down the ravine and the scary conspiracy theory is nowhere near as terrifying as reality.

We have faced monumental challenges before as a nation. We have met terrifying moments before with bold, groundbreaking solutions—but only with leaders who were willing to take the risk to break the mold and confront head-on the forces of stagnation.

In his first inaugural address, Franklin D. Roosevelt described his greatest opposition as "nameless, unreasoning, unjustified terror which paralyzes needed efforts to convert retreat into advance." He was talking during the banking crisis that had already wiped out twenty-four thousand banks and threatened another eleven thousand, at a time when unemployment was hitting more than one-fourth of the working population. "The only thing we have to fear is fear itself," he declared.

With that, he promised to wage war on the economic emergency, and he acted as if it were a life-or-death struggle. In his first hundred days, he passed fifteen major pieces of legislation in addition to ninety-nine executive orders. The reason the hundred-day mark remains so important to new presidencies is because of FDR's bold and sweeping agenda, which he called, famously, the New Deal.

It was the fourth year of the Great Depression, not the start of the nation's suffering. Four years of small government and timidity had been nowhere near enough to meet the moment. FDR didn't just prop up the banks, he put people back to work with a series of public works projects, supported farmers, and even repealed Prohibition—because you can't easily smear someone as a socialist when he has legalized beer.

That's why so many Democrats so readily signed up to the broad package of policies called the Green New Deal in 2019. While the covid-19 pandemic halted its momentum, its scale and breadth helped drive Biden's Inflation Reduction Act three years later. The Green New Deal called for a ten-year transition to 100 percent clean power generation and clean-energy transport, as well as the upgrading of buildings and infrastructure. Its goals were even more sweeping, including guaranteeing jobs, health care, and high-quality education for all.

In February 2019, Trump tweeted that the Green New Deal was a plan "to permanently eliminate all Planes, Cars, Cows, Oil, Gas & the Military." Which somehow was even more ambitious—and totally fabricated.

Trump will leave office a full decade after Representative Alexandria Ocasio-Cortez of New York and Senator Ed Markey of Massachusetts introduced their Green New Deal resolution in Congress. The world of politics has changed in that time, along with the climate crisis itself. Today only 12 percent of Americans think like Trump that global warming will never happen, according to Gallup polls. Almost two-thirds think that it's already begun. Three-quarters say that human activity has contributed to climate change either in part or greatly, according to other polling by Pew Research Center. A clear majority—64 percent—think that climate change is already affecting their local community. Similar numbers of Americans think that big businesses and the government are doing too little to reduce the impact of climate change. Huge majorities want to see corporations taxed on the basis of their carbon emissions and tax credits for homeowners to improve their homes' energy efficiency. We've moved far beyond the need for platitudes and general statements. The American people are not unsure about whether climate change is real. Trump can count on only 12 percent of the population who believe, as he does, that climate change is a con job.

A true FDR-style approach to our climate crisis would include retooling FEMA to get ahead of natural disasters, rather than just responding to them after the fact. It would build on the historic role of the U.S. Army Corps of Engineers, which has traditionally led major civil works such as flood control and large infrastructure projects. It would treat climate change as a core national security threat both at home and overseas, as it was in the Obama years.

It's not as though we can avoid paying for the climate crisis if we just pretend that it doesn't exist. Before its data tracking capability was closed down, NOAA found that the biggest extreme-weather disasters had cost the country on average $140 billion each year for the last decade. The Congressional Budget Office estimates that climate change will reduce our annual economic growth by 4 percent by the end of this century, representing trillions of dollars of losses.

Trump has perversely shown progressives the way forward. He has coerced every federal agency, many state and local governments, and numerous private institutions and major corporations to follow his lead on an entirely fabricated set of race-based crises: from immigration to diversity, equity, and inclusion.

Imagine what a newly elected, FDR-style president could achieve in combating the real and present crisis that truly affects the survival and security of our country and planet. Imagine how many jobs could be created by the green energy sector and the huge investments that would support it. If anything demands a national call to action, it's the climate crisis that is already upon us.

You don't need to be really good at predicting things to know that. You just need to live in a democracy that cares more about the future of its people than about fooling as many people as possible.

11

Lawfare

The Justice Department was so proudly independent during the Clinton years that it assigned more than 120 attorneys and FBI agents to investigate foreign contributions to the 1996 Clinton campaign. It appointed an independent counsel to investigate a failed real estate investment by the Clintons. His name was Kenneth Starr, and his digging eventually led to the impeachment of President Clinton for his affair with Monica Lewinsky. Yes, that's right. The Clinton administration was responsible for the investigation that led to Clinton's impeachment.

Skip ahead a few years to another Democratic administration. The Biden Justice Department was so principled about keeping its distance from the White House that it continued a Trump-era investigation into the sitting president's son, Hunter Biden. Attorney General Merrick Garland named a US attorney, who had first been appointed by Trump, as special counsel to pursue any wrongdoing by Hunter. In the final year of Biden's presidency, the Justice Department successfully prosecuted the president's son on felony charges for illegally purchasing a gun while he was addicted to drugs. Hunter also pleaded guilty to nine federal tax charges. The Biden Justice Department prosecuted the president's son.

There's a good reason why the Justice Department acted so independently for so long. It wasn't just to avoid the appearance of a Nixon-like scandal. The power of federal prosecutors is both great and open to abuse. It needs to be seen as evenhanded and unbiased, or else the rule of law will be undermined. As the founding father John Adams said, the United States is "a government of laws and not of men."

That was the guiding principle of Griffin Bell, attorney general in the Carter administration, who on September 6, 1978, spelled out the department's position and values in the Great Hall of the Department of Justice Building, in front of two seminaked statues. His speech was titled "Independence of the Department of Justice" because he said that the department should be "a neutral zone in the Government, because the law has to be neutral, and in our form of government there are things that are nonpartisan, and one is the law." Among his principles was that prosecutions should be decided by the various assistant attorneys general, who needed to be "insulated from influences that should not affect decisions." Those influences included "all communications about particular cases" from Congress or the White House.

"Our notions of fairness must not change from case to case," he said, "they must not be influenced by partisanship, or the privileged social, political or interest-group position of either the individuals involved in particular cases, or those who may seek to intervene against them or on their behalf."

For the best part of five decades, those principles held true. Justice needed to be seen to be done.

That is, until Trump took power. In Trump's second coming, the Justice Department as we knew it was destroyed within months, along with the values and practices that have been foundational for our democracy. The days are long gone when an attorney general talked about the neutral zone of justice, approved the investigation of a sitting president's campaign, or—God forbid—prosecuted the president's son.

The half-century-long culture of the Justice Department did not depend on a speech or a memo or a code of conduct. It survived because of its people. Under Trump, those people have been chased or pushed out the door. In the first six months of Trump's second term, around 5,500 people quit the Justice Department, were fired, or took a buyout. That included thousands of attorneys who have not been replaced, according to the advocacy group Justice Connection. The number of recent law graduates applying for jobs has also plummeted, according to the top-ranked law schools. It's hard to believe that the next generation of attorneys and prosecutors aren't knocking down the doors to work for an agency that is currently engaged in a cover-up of the most notorious pedophile ring in US history.

Jeanine Pirro, the former Fox News pundit who, because we are living in Hell, is now somehow the US Attorney for DC, told her old friends at Fox News that her office was down ninety prosecutors. She asked lawyers to email her if they wanted a job. It's the same story in Chicago, where US Attorney Andrew Boutros emailed former prosecutors, asking them to consider applying for jobs in his office and to forward his email to any friends who might be interested.

These jobs used to be some of the most desirable opportunities in the legal profession. Instead, top lawyers are applying for state government positions, according to the American Bar Association. The Trump administration has been left to fill its vacancies with more political activists than in the past: people with law degrees who are working in congressional offices and advocacy groups. Or they are hiring lawyers with no background in prosecutions and no experience of the independent culture of the Justice Department. To help with their goal of politicizing justice, they are now asking job applicants to list a Trump executive order or policy that is significant to them and explain how they would advance it. The object is clear: This administration wants as prosecutors Trump loyalists and ideologues who will push forward his agenda, not enforce the laws with impartiality.

Nowhere is the collapse of justice more obvious than in the Civil Rights Division, where the vast majority of its six hundred employees—including more than 70 percent of its lawyers—have left. As its name suggests, the division was created during the civil rights era to combat discrimination. For the last six decades, it has worked to protect the constitutional rights of all Americans on everything from voting to housing, jobs, schools, and policing.

That's all gone. Today its role is to enforce Trump's war on woke: attacking civil rights policies for supposedly victimizing white folks, attacking schools for pursuing diversity and inclusion, attacking anyone who supports transgender rights, and pursuing something called anti-Christian bias. It's a perversion of civil rights, and it's entirely intentional. The new head of the division is Harmeet Dhillon, a former Republican official and regular guest on Fox News. She explained her approach to the conservative Federalist Society by saying that Democratic administrations were like a speeding train on civil rights, and previous Republican administrations had just been trying to slow down the train. "There really hasn't been a focus on turning the train around and driving it in the opposite direction. And that's my vision of the DOJ civil rights [division]," she said. "We don't just slow down the woke. We take up the cause to achieve the executive branch's goals. This is the opportunity where we can ensure that our nation's civil rights laws benefit all Americans, not just a select few."

Except that's not the point of civil rights laws. And it's not the effect of her approach to the Civil Rights Division. Dhillon issued new mission statements that include "Protecting Children from Chemical and Surgical Mutilation" and "Keeping Men Out of Women's Sports." Among the dozens of cases that have been twisted to the point of incoherence, there's one that involves firefighters in Georgia. Black and white people were applying for positions in the Cobb County fire department at the same rate, but 90 percent of hires were white. When the Civil Rights Division asked for an explanation, the fire department said that Black people had more student debt, so they might steal from a fire victim's home. Within a month of taking office, Trump's lapdog of an attorney general, Pam Bondi, didn't just want to withdraw the case. No, she wanted to state that the case was actually about discriminating against *white* people. The Civil Rights Division lawyers refused to sign her order and expected to be fired. In the end, their boss signed a modified version on their behalf to save their jobs.

That's not even the most political of all the Trumpifications of the Justice Department. That prize surely belongs to the purging of dozens of prosecutors who worked on the hundreds of criminal cases involving the insurrection at the Capitol on January 6, 2021. It wasn't enough to pardon hardened criminals who viciously attacked police officers. Pardoning crimes undermines the law, but nothing destroys the law like firing government lawyers who are just doing their job of prosecuting criminals. During the four-year investigation of the riot, hundreds of prosecutors from across the country were involved in the 1,600 criminal cases. Deputy Attorney General Emil Bove claimed that the purge had not been about January 6 but had simply targeted people improperly hired by the Biden administration. Sure, and the No Kings protests weren't about Trump's overreach but merely an innocent commentary on the monarchical system of government of our forebears.

Bove knows something about questionable hiring practices. Prior to joining the Justice Department as its number two in command, he was Trump's personal lawyer as part of the criminal defense team in the cases involving the 2020 election results, including the January 6 insurrection. Just a few months into his reign of terror at the Justice Department, Trump appointed Bove to the appeals court in Philadelphia amid speculation that he would name him to the Supreme Court as soon as a vacancy opened up.

This is the kind of neutral, impartial lawyer that Bove is: When the courts opposed Trump's moves to deport immigrants overseas with no legal review, he told his underlings that they should ignore the courts. The deportations included Kilmar Abrego Garcia, who was flown to a prison in El Salvador along with a group of Venezuelans in defiance of a court order. The career lawyer handling the case, Erez Reuveni, told the court that the deportation had been a mistake—an admission that got him fired. He later filed a whistleblower report explaining that Bove had driven the illegal deportations despite an expected court order to halt them. "Bove stated that DOJ would need to consider telling the courts 'fuck you' and ignore any such order," Reuveni stated. ". . . Silence overtook the room."

When you demolish the independence of the Justice Department, when you politicize the prosecutors, you destroy the fundamentals of our democratic government. You end up with a federal appeals court judge—and possible future Supreme Court justice—who believes that the Justice Department can say "Fuck you" to the courts. It does not take long to slide all the way down the slippery slope to the end of the rule of law—the same rule of law that Trump once promised to protect.

* * *

The excuse for demolishing justice is that the last guys weaponized the place. So naturally, it was already demolished when they walked in the door. That plainly isn't true, but it's a useful political ruse. On the day of his second inauguration, Trump signed an executive order titled "Ending the Weaponization of the Federal Government." It builds a mountain of lies in order to justify the very behavior it condemns. Because if the other team played dirty, why shouldn't team Trump?

"The American people have witnessed the previous administration engage in a systematic campaign against its perceived political opponents, weaponizing the legal force of numerous Federal law enforcement agencies and the Intelligence Community against those perceived political opponents in the form of investigations, prosecutions, civil enforcement actions, and other related actions," the order began. "These actions appear oriented more toward inflicting political pain than toward pursuing actual justice or legitimate governmental objectives."

What have the American people witnessed? The first instance cited is "parents protesting at school board meetings." That was one of the many targets of the conspiracy-peddling House Judiciary Committee chairman, Jim Jordan. At the center of his investigation was a 2021 memo from then Attorney General Merrick Garland about "a disturbing spike in harassment, intimidation, and threats of violence against school administrators, board members, teachers, and staff" at public schools. ". . . While spirited debate about policy matters is protected under our Constitution, that protection does not extend to threats of violence or efforts to intimate individuals based on their views," Garland explained, as he asked the FBI to cooperate with state and local law enforcement.

That's exhibit A in the case for weaponization.

Trump's weaponization memo goes on to another case of right-wing violence, this one condemned by Republican leaders in Congress. "The Department of Justice has ruthlessly prosecuted more than 1,500 individuals associated with January 6, and simultaneously dropped nearly all cases against BLM rioters," Trump wrote in his executive order. It all amounted to "an unprecedented, third-world weaponization of prosecutorial power to upend the democratic process."

Let's pass over the false equivalence of the Black Lives Matter protests with an insurrection intended to overturn the results of a free and fair election and hang the then vice president. Most of the BLM cases were dropped because mass arrests had been used as crowd control and the evidence had never justified the prosecutions. In Dallas, for instance, most of the cases weren't filed because the police dropped them. Officers still sent nearly two hundred charges to the local prosecutor's office, most of which were dropped at that stage. Even in Detroit, where the mayor was a former prosecutor who wanted to make an example of the protestors, the cases amounted to low-level misdemeanors. One district judge dismissed more than a hundred cases because police refused to provide basic evidence such as body cam videos. The city ended up dropping hundreds of cases because the officers who had written tickets had not been at the protests and hadn't witnessed the supposed crimes. In New York City, the charges were so shoddy that the city agreed to pay more than $13 million to thousands of protestors who had been arrested or beaten by the city's police officers.

Those are exhibits B and C in the case for weaponization—as if hundreds of charges with no evidence are the same as the hundreds of cases that went to trial of the people who stomped on the heads of the Capitol police, beat them with metal poles, or threatened to kill the speaker of the House.

In fact, it took Biden's attorney general almost two years to appoint Jack Smith as special counsel to investigate Trump for his undemocratic attempts to overturn the 2020 election and his illegal possession of the most highly classified national security documents at Mar-a-Lago. That appointment happened only after Trump declared that he would run for the presidency again. Ironically, Merrick Garland's meticulous and protracted attempts to avoid doing anything that might look political instead looked even more political. By delaying his deliberations, he also allowed Trump to run out the clock on the investigations by mounting endless legal challenges.

Playing the victim while victimizing others has a long track record among totalitarian rulers. It clears the path for any amount of retribution, because the punishment looks like some kind of justice. The game is even more successful if you accuse your opponent of doing exactly what you're attempting to do. The layers of lying are dizzying.

That was the approach of Joseph Goebbels, the chief propagandist for the Nazi Party, who explained how it all works in a speech in Nuremburg in September 1934. "The cleverest trick used in propaganda against Germany during the war was to accuse Germany of what our enemies themselves were doing," he said, referencing World War I and its aftermath. "Even today, large parts of world opinion are convinced that the typical characteristics of German propaganda are lying, crudeness, reversing the facts, and the like. One needs only to remember the stories that were spread throughout the world at the beginning of the war about German soldiers chopping off children's hands and crucifying women to realize that Germany then was a defenseless victim of this campaign of calumny."

Victimhood is one of the most constant excuses for Russia's current aggression against Ukraine. Vladimir Putin claims that his brutal war is justified because Russia has always been a blameless victim of foreign aggression. His grievances extend back to a Polish occupation of the Kremlin in 1612, Swedish invasions in 1708, Napoleon's invasion in 1812, and the Nazi attack in 1941. Germany's invasion was the excuse Josef Stalin needed to seize Poland, the Baltic states, and Finland in the early years of World War II. The Soviets extended that excuse across Eastern Europe as the reason for controlling half of Europe throughout the Cold War.

That's the thing about dictatorships: They don't abandon all the trappings of democracy, they just twist them so far out of shape that they become meaningless. There were elections and laws in the Soviet Union. They just meant nothing that we would recognize as elections and laws. People lived in a regime in which Stalin's secret police lived by the famous saying "Give me the man and I will find the crime."

We are thankfully still a long way from totalitarianism in the United States. Comparisons with Adolf Hitler's Germany and Stalin's Soviet Union are always extreme because those regimes committed extreme atrocities. But we would be blind to history if we failed to see the warning signs in their rapid decline into dictatorship. Once the rule of law breaks down, the decline tends to speed up, not slow down.

Find the crime; that's the basis for charging ex–FBI Director James Comey and New York Attorney General Letitia James. We know that because Trump blurted out the truth on nothing less than Truth Social. The post was supposed to be a direct message to his attorney general, Pam Bondi. But seventy-nine-year-old men are not known for their mastery of technology, and Trump blasted his orders to the world beyond his cabinet of misfit toys: "Pam: I have reviewed over 30 statements and posts saying that, essentially, 'same old story as last time, all talk, no action. Nothing is being done. What about Comey,

Adam "Shifty" Schiff, Leticia??? They're all guilty as hell, but nothing is going to be done,'" Trump wrote, before explaining that he had fired a US attorney in Virginia because he wouldn't prosecute. He continued, "There is a GREAT CASE, and many lawyers, and legal pundits, say so. Lindsey Halligan is a really good lawyer, and likes you, a lot. We can't delay any longer, it's killing our reputation and credibility. They impeached me twice, and indicted me (5 times!), OVER NOTHING. JUSTICE MUST BE SERVED, NOW!!!" In case Bondi was confused about who was issuing the marching orders, he signed the post "President DJT."

Sometimes the criminal fraternity just can't help but give themselves away. Trump is no exception.

James Comey was indicted by a grand jury on charges that he made a false statement to Congress and obstructed a congressional proceeding. The alleged lie was that he had told a hearing that he had not authorized someone at the FBI to leak information about investigations into the 2016 election that Trump won—in particular, about Russian interference and Hillary Clinton's use of a private email server. But really, his crime was that he had investigated Russian support for Trump in that election.

Letitia James was indicted by a grand jury on one charge of bank fraud and one count of making a false statement to a financial institution. Those charges were based on an accusation of committing mortgage fraud when she purchased a home in Virginia and said it was a second home instead of an investment property. In reality, the mortgage contract expressly allowed her to rent out the home. Her actual crime was securing a $500 million fraud judgment against Trump and his companies because they had lied to the banks and insurers about the value of their properties. Sometimes they were inflated, sometimes deflated—depending on whether the Trump businesses were borrowing money or trying to minimize their interest payments. Now, that's what you call bank fraud.

The only thing standing in the way of Trump's vindictive prosecutions was the good lawyers of the Justice Department. So when Erik

Siebert, the US attorney for the Eastern District of Virginia, couldn't find enough evidence to charge Comey and James, he quit. Siebert was not some Democratic holdover; he had come recommended by Virginia's Republican governor and had worked closely with Trump's former lawyer Emil Bove on immigration cases.

His replacement was another of Trump's personal lawyers, who had started working for him after they met at his golf club in 2021. She had worked as part of his defense team on the cases involving his attempt to overturn the 2020 election, as well as the highly classified documents he illegally stashed at Mar-a-Lago. She was just a low-level White House staffer when Trump told Bondi that she was a really good lawyer and that she liked her. A lot.

Lindsey Halligan had no prosecutorial experience, but that wasn't nearly as important as her loyalty to Trump—at least in Trump's eyes. For the federal courts, her incompetence and her appointment were problems. She ignored the findings of federal prosecutors and investigators that there was insufficient evidence to charge Comey. A magistrate judge found that she made at least two "fundamental and highly prejudicial" misstatements in front of the grand jury, including her suggestion that Comey didn't have the right under the Fifth Amendment to avoid testifying at his own trial. She also screwed up her attempts to turn a three-count indictment into two charges, presenting different indictments to the grand jury and the court. Those basic procedural mistakes were compounded by the illegal status of her own position. A federal judge threw out the cases against Comey and James because she was "unlawfully serving" as an interim US attorney. A new grand jury refused to indict James at the second attempt.

Halligan wasn't the only illegal prosecutor on Team Trump. A week after a judge threw out Halligan's cases, a federal appeals court found that Alina Habba, another of Trump's personal lawyers, was serving unlawfully as US attorney, this time in New Jersey. Like Halligan, Habba had no experience in criminal law and had been named to the position without the required Senate approval. In all, judges found that five US attorneys were serving unlawfully as of early 2026.

This poses a question about the competence of the person at the top of Trump's pretend prosecutors: Attorney General Pam Bondi. In Trump's first term, his attorneys general felt some kind of kinship to the values and principles of the Justice Department, tortured and dwindling though it may be. His first appointment, Senator Jeff Sessions of Alabama, recused himself from the Russia investigation, leading to the appointment of Robert Mueller as special prosecutor. His second attorney general, William Barr, refused to join in Trump's attempts to overturn the 2020 election.

In his second term, Trump first chose Matt Gaetz as his attorney general, but that was a bridge too far even for the MAGA sycophants on Capitol Hill. Quite apart from the ethics investigation into Gaetz's drugs and sex life (which wasn't necessarily a deal breaker), he had made sworn enemies inside his own party across Congress (which was).

Bondi was Trump's second choice but checked the same, vital box: undying loyalty to Trump. As Florida attorney general, she had been the first major state official to endorse Trump in 2016 after Jeb Bush, a former governor, had pulled out. She had spoken at the Republican National Convention in 2016, celebrating its mob chants to lock up Hillary Clinton. She was fully on board with Trump's attempted coup in 2020 and even stood with Rudy Giuliani at his genius press conference at Four Seasons Total Landscaping in Philadelphia, the store between a sex shop and a crematorium—surely a highlight of any lawyer's career. When Trump was indicted for his role in trying to overturn the 2020 election, Bondi went on Fox News to promise that when Trump returned to power, "the prosecutors will be prosecuted, the bad ones." Along the way, she earned $1 million from a Trump-linked lobbying firm, $525,000 from a Trump-linked think tank, and 3 million shares in Trump Media, which runs Truth Social. She may be a trashy lawyer, but she's a world-class grifter.

At an early cabinet meeting, Bondi led the charge in North Korean–style sycophancy that still has the power to horrify the sane world. "President," she began in her peculiarly childish way, "your first hundred days has far exceeded that of any other presidency in this country ever, ever. Never seen anything like it. Thank you." She claimed bizarrely that they had saved the lives of most of the entire American population thanks to her department's drug busts. "Since you have been in office, President Trump, your DOJ agencies have seized more than 22 million fentanyl pills, 3,400 kilos of fentanyl since your last 100 days. Which saved—are you ready for this, media?—258 million lives."

There are 342 million Americans, so it's just as well that Bondi managed to save the country from an extinction-level event like that. Unless she completely misunderstood those numbers.

The Justice Department might be able to survive an incompetent and obsequious attorney general if the deputy in charge were halfway decent. Sadly, he isn't. Todd Blanche defended Trump in his criminal trial in 2024 in New York regarding hush money paid to a porn star in 2016. The defense failed, making Trump the first former president in history to be convicted of felony crimes. It was Blanche who interviewed Ghislaine Maxwell in prison as the administration struggled to fulfill its promise to release all the files related to Jeffrey Epstein, who just happened to be an old friend of one Donald Trump. It was another triumph of lawyering, which did nothing to stop the Epstein sewage lapping at Trump's feet.

That's not to say that Blanche is totally useless. He's an Olympic-level gymnast when it comes to flipping the truth into a somersault of lies. "What happened the past four years within the United States Department of Justice, I'm going to say a Latin term: batshit crazy," he told the right-wing lawyers at the Federalist Society in November 2025. "When I read now that we're weaponizing, I feel like I'm being gaslit, because we're doing exactly the opposite. I take umbrage at the idea that the work that our prosecutors are doing is weaponization, because I have receipts. I know what happened the past couple years. I've lived it."

Winston Churchill supposedly said, "Anyone can rat, but it takes a certain amount of ingenuity to re-rat." If only he'd been alive to see the Trump gang at work. Because anyone can gaslight. But it takes a certain amount of ingenuity to gaslight about gaslighting.

Here's a receipt that Todd Blanche should look at. There's a guy named Paul Ingrassia, who was nominated to lead the Office of Special Counsel. It's a big legal job inside the federal government, with prosecutorial powers, whose main job is to protect employees from reprisals for whistleblowing. That covers the really bad stuff government officials might be doing, such as engaging in corruption, abusing power, wasting money, or doing political campaigning. Kind of Trumpy stuff.

Ingrassia was not just obviously unqualified for the job; he had worked as White House liaison to the Justice Department with a mission to hire people based on what he called "exceptional loyalty" to Trump. In his zealous hunt for absolute submission, he managed to clash with Bondi's chief of staff. He even told Trump directly that Bondi's team was hurting the president. That won him lots of enemies. But it was nothing compared to the text messages he sent to a group of Republicans, including his admission that he had "a Nazi streak" and hated the national holiday celebrating the birthday of Martin Luther King, Jr. Politico's reporting about his racist texts led several Republican senators, including Senate Majority Leader John Thune, to say that Ingrassia's nomination would not be confirmed.

Soon after the White House pulled the plug on his nomination, new reporting emerged from ProPublica about Ingrassia. Back in the White House as liaison with the Department of Homeland Security, Ingrassia intervened on behalf of the accused sex traffickers Andrew Tate and his brother, Tristan, to have their phones returned to them after they were seized in Fort Lauderdale by US Customs and Border Protection. Ingrassia had previously worked at a law firm that just happened to represent the Tate brothers.

It's the kind of unethical abuse of power that a whistleblower would bring to public attention—if whistleblowers were still safe in Trump's America.

* * *

What does reform look like the day after Trump? Cleaning up our politics after years of lawlessness and corruption must start with law enforcement. You don't need a law degree to understand the scandal around the dropping of corruption charges against New York City Mayor Eric Adams. Trump's desire for loyalty, for government officials to follow his orders blindly—including those on his immigration raids in New York, for instance—is itself a corrupting influence on public service. That's why the interim US attorney and several other public integrity lawyers quit their jobs because of the Adams case. Corrupt officials hate the rule of law because it cramps their corruption.

Restoring the rule of law starts with accountability for the corrupt officials who have perverted public service into a private profit machine. Inside the new Justice department, there will need to be a special unit of prosecutors and investigators tasked with pursuing corruption cases throughout the Trump years. Not just to deliver justice to criminals, but to deter future corruption in later administrations. There were hundreds of prosecutors involved in the cases surrounding the January 6 insurrection. The corruption prosecutions for crimes committed during the second Trump term will surely involve similar numbers of prosecutors. However, they must move with more speed and determination than the Biden Justice department. Merrick Garland put optics above justice; the opposite approach must be taken by the next Democratic attorney general.

Judicial review has protected the functioning of some US attorneys; it should extend to all US attorneys. Those court protections should extend to special counsels, so that they can be removed only "for good cause" when the cause can be proved before a judge. The same is true for the head of the Office of Special Counsel, to protect whistleblowers across the board.

Restoring the rule of law means reforming government to root out corruption. Congress could start by reforming the Office of

Government Ethics, whose role is confined to issuing rules and regulations regarding standards of conduct and conflicts of interest. A new reform-minded Congress should give the ethics office real teeth by granting it the power to investigate ethics violations and bring civil cases to court. To avoid Trump's blanket firings of disloyal agency heads, Congress should protect the head of the ethics office from being fired except for good cause—and good cause should be specified clearly, or else mortgage paperwork will be used as an excuse once again.

Congress needs to beef up protections for the inspectors general who were pushed out or silenced in Trump's second term. That should include giving them the power to investigate White House interactions with law enforcement.

Above all, Congress needs to write into law the voluntary principles established after the Nixon years about the protection of the Justice Department from political interference. Congress must require each administration to publish its policy on contact with law enforcement agencies and log those contacts when they take place. Those logs need to be reported regularly to the House and Senate committees overseeing the Justice Department.

To that end, it should set up a special investigation into Trump's corruption of law enforcement—much like the Church Committee investigation into intelligence agency abuses after the Nixon years—so there is a full accounting and understanding of what has taken place.

Trump has destroyed the independence of federal prosecutors. He has profited from the partisan power grab on the Supreme Court, destroying the independence of the courts. He has even bullied the biggest law firms into surrender. Reviving a sense of independence is not going to be simple.

The United States of America is a country of laws, whose founding documents are displayed as national treasures in the rotunda of the National Archives. Restoring respect for those laws is not just a matter of passing laws; it's about restoring our culture and identity, of remembering who we are as Americans and why we cling so tightly to our Constitution.

Without the rule of law, the American project is finished. We cannot afford to let that happen for the profit of one corrupt president and the sycophantic cult that surrounds him.

Epilogue

The forty-eighth president of the United States will need a super-human level of political courage. It's not a job for a frail or feeble spirit. There's no middle ground when it comes to restoring our democracy after four years of unbridled attacks. There's no compromise when it comes to cleaning up after such lawless corruption.

That's if we're fortunate enough to have a free and fair election in 2028 that results in a Democratic president at all.

If there is a peaceful transition of power, the temptation to revert back to the old ways will be strong. It's easier, for sure, to do less. The political establishment will be exhausted by the pace of change. Incremental steps will feel like a relief. They can always be justified by a comforting bedtime story that people just want to return to normal, boring, small-time politics, the kind that doesn't blow up your news alerts every single day. It is, after all, in part what landed Joe Biden in the White House after Trump's first term.

But that's not what people want. They are deeply, deeply unhappy with the status quo. They are deeply, deeply unhappy with the Trumpian revolution. Neither of those versions of American power solved their core problems. Neither of those versions of American power changed their disdain for self-serving, corrupt officials.

You don't need to spend millions of dollars on polling to know what the core problems are. The cost of living is too high. The middle class has been squeezed by rising costs, stagnant wages, unstable jobs, and a deadlocked housing market. That's been the story of the last two or three decades. We want an economy that works for us. We don't want to work for the economy. That means a minimum wage that is a living wage. That means a health care system that won't bankrupt us and that actually makes us healthy. That means living in a neighborhood that isn't at risk of being destroyed by floods or fires, by a climate that's spiraling out of control. Until our leaders can deliver on those basic needs, they are destined to fail. They will be tarnished with the same distrust as all the others who preceded them: the MAGA loyalists and the moderates, all of them lumped together in a cesspool of corruption and cluelessness.

Until we elect a president who understands the scale of the challenge and the gravity of the moment, this country—and the other countries that follow its lead—will be stuck in its current doom loop.

Our system needs to be reformed so that it can deliver the changes we are crying out for. That means reforming the Supreme Court. It means reforming the Senate to end the filibuster. It means reforming the powers of the presidency, government checks and balances, and the power of prosecutors. It means wielding power—in a *virtuous* way—so that our democracy can endure.

Above all, it means recognizing that we have already passed the tipping point of autocracy. We can pretend that it's not happening. We can tell ourselves that it's just a phase. We can remember all those times when the idea of America was an inspiration to the world. But we know we're fooling ourselves. We know that the reality is overwhelming in scale and scope. We know that denial is not a solution; it's a coping mechanism.

The first stage of recovery is to admit that our democracy is failing. The second stage is to make an inventory of our failures, being honest about the root causes. Those failures are not just the result of the enemies of democracy; they are also the result of the complacent friends of democracy, who have been too fearful to take action. The third stage is to seek accountability for those who have corrupted our system and abused power, because there can be no reform without a full reckoning. The fourth stage is to deliver results for the people who empower our leaders. Fixing the system matters only if the system improves the lives of our families, friends, and neighbors.

The day after Trump leaves the White House will present a unique and brief opportunity in our history. There won't be another moment quite like it. The forces of reform will be united, briefly, in the expectation of radical change. There's a reason why FDR could push through so many changes in his first hundred days—because everything gets harder after that.

If the forty-eighth president does not seize the moment and pursue root-and-branch reform, to deliver on the promise of America, we are destined to see our republic slide into terminal decline. There can be no more sacred cows after four years of Trump's demolition of the temples of democracy. It has taken decades of plotting and scheming to bring us to this point. We no longer have decades to arrest the decline.

Our last chance to save democracy is upon us. It's not somebody else's job. We need to be ready to write the history that future generations will celebrate. The day after Trump is the first day of the America we always knew we could build.

ACKNOWLEDGMENTS

The irony of working in digital media is that I have the immense privilege of being able to reach millions of people every day—and the disadvantage of doing so too often in complete solitude. This book, in its collaboration with so many kind, talented people, offered a rare and welcome respite from the isolation. Without them, *The Day After* wouldn't be even half the book it is.

I must first thank Richard Wolffe, whose remarkable wealth of knowledge, mastery of the craft, and quick wit is felt on every page. I am endlessly fortunate to have had the opportunity to work with someone whose passion is so evident. The success of this book belongs every bit as much to Richard as it does to myself.

To Sean Desmond, my editor, your kindness, optimism, and calm I am both envious of and grateful for. I am beyond appreciative of the faith you have in me as an author. Thank you, as always, for making what should be a daunting process such an easy one. Although you're the only publisher with whom I've worked, I am acutely aware of how spoiled I am. And to the rest of the HarperCollins team—publishers, editors, copyeditors, production, marketing, publicity, design, art, audio, and anyone else I might have missed—thank you for making this process so seamless and this book such a success.

My team at UTA—Marc Paskin, Pilar Queen, Dan Milaschewski—believed in me long, long before I believed in myself. Thank you for fielding my (anxious) calls, navigating my (anxious) requests, and dealing with my (anxious) anxiety. I truly could not have a better team. Thank you for your kindness, your help, and your friendship. And Marc, I promise I will not forget to eat. But please don't stop reminding me.

Thank you to those who spared their valuable time to share their ideas with me for this book. Senator Bernie Sanders and Senator Elizabeth Warren: It's an honor to be able to say that you were a part of this project. Thank you for fighting relentlessly to make this country a more just, fair, and decent place. Glenn Kirschner, my longtime partner and friend, your passion for justice is contagious, and this country is better off for your service to it. And finally, I owe a special debt of gratitude to Marc Elias, hero of democracy and my friend, for writing the foreword for this book. History will remember the work you are doing to protect this country and its ideals. I am so, so proud that your name appears on the cover.

None of what I do on a daily basis would be possible without my own amazing team: Drew, Dillon, Luke, Parker, Lauren, Nick, Stuart, Daniel, Adam, Hallie, and Sam. You all do the work of way too many people—and you do it way too well. Thank you.

To the Chorus team and creators: Thank you for doing the hard work every single day to strengthen the pro-democracy ecosystem. I'm so grateful to work alongside you and proud of the difference you're making.

To my parents, family, and girlfriend, your love and support means everything to me (even if much of it is encouraging much-needed breaks that I refuse to take). How lucky I am to have a support system made of steel. To Lisa, thank you for the years of inspiration and advice. And to my dog, Aston, my sweet boy, thank you for being a boundless source of joy.

But most importantly, I must recognize everyone staying involved, staying engaged, and meeting this moment with the urgency it deserves. As we read about other defining moments in history, we often think about how we might have acted if we'd been there. This is one of those moments. Those who are standing up, speaking out, and fighting back are the people whom history will remember. Benjamin Franklin famously said of our new country, "A republic, if you can keep it." We can—and we will.

Defense, Department of, 149
defense budget, 18
Defense of Marriage Act, 23
deficits, 24, 32, 43, 104
Delaware, 35, 55
democracy, x, xii, 7, 10, 15, 21, 28, 34, 45, 53, 55, 56, 69, 70, 72, 74, 75, 77, 83–86, 95, 97, 101, 114, 117, 140, 151, 184–85
Democracy Watch podcast, xi
Democratic National Convention of 2004, 25
Democratic Party, xi, 15, 16, 23, 28–40, 50, 53–55, 61, 71, 73–81, 83, 105–8, 114–16, 121, 122, 131, 134, 139, 164, 169
Dempsey, David, 95–96
deportations, 19, 170–71
DeSantis, Ron, 82
Dhillon, Harmeet, 169
discrimination, 12, 13
Disney, Walt, 9
diversity, equality, and inclusion (DEI) initiatives, 9, 19, 126, 165
Dole, Bob, 33, 34
Dominion Voting Systems, 19
"Don't ask, don't tell" policy, 23
Doocy, Steve, 142
Douglas, Stephen A., 36
Dred Scott decision (1857), 68
due process, 14, 68

early voting, 56, 83
Eastman, John, 96
economy, 103–11, 113, 116, 150
Education, Department of, 19, 36
education reform, 36
Eisenhower, Dwight D., 8–9
El Salvador, 170
elections (*see* midterm elections; presidential elections)
Electoral College, 66, 74, 85, 96
electric vehicles, 153–54, 161
Elias, Marc, ix–xii
Ellison, David, 18, 145–46
Ellison, Larry, 145
Emanuel, Rahm, 29
Energy, Department of, 159
environmental issues, 11, 30, 154–55, 158, 160, 161, 164
Environmental Protection Agency (EPA), 159
Epshteyn, Boris, 96

Epstein, Jeffrey, 51, 153, 178
Equal Employment Opportunity Commission, 12
Equal Pay Act of 1963, 13
Equal Rights Amendment, 13
Erdogan, Recep Tayyip, 149
Ethics in Government Act of 1978, 98

Facebook, 150
Fairness Doctrine, 140–41
fascism, 134, 138, 140
FBI (Federal Bureau of Investigation), 44, 47, 77, 172, 175
FCC (Federal Communications Commission), 133–34, 136–41, 144, 150
federal judges, 63, 64
Federal Reserve, 20, 50
Federalist Society, 63, 66, 169
FEMA (Federal Emergency Management Agency), 159, 162, 165
Feminine Mystique, The (Friedan), 12–13
feminism, 12–13
Fifth Amendment to the Constitution, 59, 176
filibuster, 35, 42–43, 54–56, 70, 81, 83, 101, 116, 184
financial crisis of 2008, 26, 40, 104
Fiore, Michele, 92–93
First Amendment to the Constitution, 135, 137, 138
Fix the Court, 66
flooding, 162–63
Florida, 21, 25, 74, 82, 116
Floyd, George, 91
Ford, Gerald, 92
Fortas, Abe, 16
Foster, Vince, 19
Fourteenth Amendment to the Constitution, 14, 68
Fourth Amendment to the Constitution, 58, 59, 60
Fox News, 39, 47, 58, 96, 107, 135, 140, 142, 145, 148, 149, 168, 169, 177
Fox News Radio, 144
Freedom of Information Act of 1966, 98
Freedom to Vote Act of 2021, 56, 83–84, 86
Friedan, Betty, 12
Frimpong, Maame, 59
Fuentes, Nick, 13

Gaetz, Matt, 177
Garcia, Kilmar Abrego, 63, 170